State F
D0534461

Ron Schara's
Minnesota

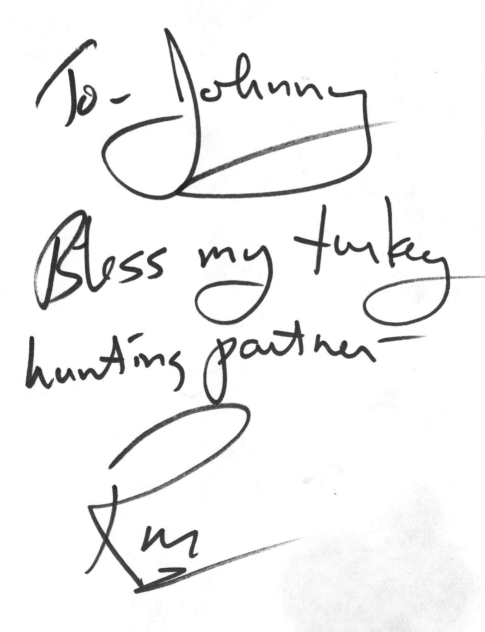

To - Johnny

Bless my turkey

hunting partner -

Ron

Struktur 2021

16 - Johann

Klass mu tuke

hunting gartin

Ron Schara's
Minnesota

Mostly True Tales of a
Life Outdoors

RON SCHARA

**MINNESOTA
HISTORICAL
SOCIETY PRESS**

Ron Schara is a former employee of Star Tribune Media Company LLC in Minneapolis, Minnesota. Some of the articles in this book were first published in the *Star Tribune* newspaper or on StarTribune.com. Those articles and photos are copyright by Star Tribune Media Company LLC and are reprinted here with permission. Star Tribune retains all copyright and syndication rights for those articles and photos.

Other text and images copyright © 2021 by Ron Schara. Additional materials copyright © 2021 by the Minnesota Historical Society. All rights reserved. No part of this book may be used or reproduced in any manner whatsoever without written permission except in the case of brief quotations embodied in critical articles and reviews. For information, write to the Minnesota Historical Society Press, 345 Kellogg Blvd. W., St. Paul, MN 55102–1906.

mnhspress.org

The Minnesota Historical Society Press is a member of the Association of University Presses.

Manufactured in the United States of America

10 9 8 7 6 5 4 3 2 1

♾ The paper used in this publication meets the minimum requirements of the American National Standard for Information Sciences—Permanence for Printed Library Materials, ANSI Z39.48–1984.

International Standard Book Number
ISBN: 978-1-68134-192-7 (paper)
ISBN: 978-1-68134-193-4 (e-book)

Library of Congress Control Number: 2021930817

This and other Minnesota Historical Society Press books are available from popular e-book vendors.

To Denise, who for more than half a century
kept the home fires burning while I ventured
far and wide in search of the next story.

To my daughters, Simone and Laura,
who have grown into women with their own
hopes and dreams, including the next fish,
the next pheasant, the next wild turkey.

To grandson Jake, who at age eight
easily whacked my pitched tennis balls
into the Rum River and who at age fourteen
followed his grandpa in pursuit of gobblers.
Now as a young man, Jake follows his own dreams,
which include whacking home runs in the major leagues.

CONTENTS

FOREWORD

If you don't want to be forgotten as soon as you are dead, either write things worth reading or do things worth writing about.
   —Benjamin Franklin

On the pages up ahead is my life. Well, okay, not all of my living days, but many of them. After all, for more than half a century I've been gathering stories from all corners of Minnesota and neighboring states, plus wild places elsewhere in North America, including duck swamps in Canada and distant lands—from the plains of South Africa to Brazil's Amazon River to Norway's Arctic Circle, where I was fishing on September 11, 2001.

This book was not meant to be about me. For that reason, details of my life, the joys and the sorrows, the wins and the losses, the whining and the gloating are not included. In these pages are my stories as told by me with, at times, a little journalistic license included here and there.

For example, my Uncle Harvey Dickens, one of my mom's brothers, really wasn't the family hillbilly in the pure sense of the word. He was a wonderful uncle who sent me fancy silk Japanese jackets and handmade bamboo fly rods from Japan during his army days in the Korean War. However, Uncle Harvey was dumb like a fox, just like a hillbilly might be. Here's how: He was a rattlesnake hunter in northeast Iowa. Back then, the only good timber rattlesnake was a dead one. The local county paid a bounty (don't remember how much) for every rattlesnake tail brought to the courthouse. Like I said, Uncle Harvey was no dummy. When he caught a female rattler who was ready to give birth, Uncle Harvey kept her alive in an empty horse tank. When the babies were born, the tails of mother snake and baby snakes all went to the courthouse for bounty money.

Hey, a man's gotta make a living, which included being a penny pincher. The last time Uncle Harvey and I fished together for walleyes on Serpent Lake at Crosby, Minnesota, the end of his fishing line was a sight to behold. Hook, line, and . . . his sinkers once were nuts from some unknown machines. RIP, Uncle Harvey.

As I reviewed and reread the stories in these pages, I noticed a few trends that sadden me to this day. Often I wrote about losses or degradation of boyhood haunts. Nothing stays the same, I know. In this case, however, the changes were for the worse. And you feel shame and pain because the next generation will not have what you had.

When I began writing about wildlife and about hunting, there was no animal rights movement—just a few "little ol' ladies in tennis shoes," as they were often described. Those are not my words. Nevertheless, more and more Americans began to subscribe to the concept of animal rights and began to demand more humane treatment of animals on the farm or at packing plants. Often, it was the right thing to do.

It didn't stop there, however. America's hunters and wildlife agencies also became targets of criticism by animal rights advocates who claimed hunting wasn't necessary anymore; sport hunting was just "killing for fun." Wearing animal fur also was proclaimed a sin; trapping was cruel and unnecessary, they said.

As the outdoor columnist for the *Minneapolis Tribune*, what was I to do? Wade into the debate, of course. A debate that naturally became endless. I don't regret opposing animal rights positions or the hate mail that followed my criticisms. As an Iowa State University graduate—studying fish and wildlife biology combined with journalism—I found the hypocrisy so inherent in animal rights protests simply could not be ignored.

We should stop wearing fur, the animal rights extremists demanded. Fur is an animal's skin with the hair on it. Nothing was said about wearing animal skins with the hair removed, such as leather shoes and leather coats. I wondered: *What would the Holstein cow say about this? It's okay to wear my skin on your shoulders but not that of the mink?* Is a cow's life less sacred than a mink's?

Eating wild game was cruel too, they claimed. We should eat

plants, not animals. What? Where do our plants come from? The answer is from fields that once were homes to wildlife, homes eliminated when the plows moved in. Clearing fields for vegetables, using chemicals and so forth may be more damaging to all wildlife than a hunter's gun. Nobody talks about that.

Okay, enough. Hunting and animal rights are here to stay. Can't we just get along?

Sometimes my stories stirred my own passions. When I discovered the joy of hunting wild turkeys, my life was forever changed. I was inspired to start the first Minnesota chapter of the National Wild Turkey Federation and become its first president. We led the effort to restore wild turkeys in Minnesota.

I watched the first Ducks Unlimited chapter in action. Hunters determined to improve the lives of waterfowl and themselves. I helped start the second DU chapter in Rochester, where I knew a foot doctor, Dr. Bob Sabbann, who cherished duck hunting and agreed to help.

I watched duck hunters from Albert Lea who could not stand to see their waterfowl lakes decline, wild-eyed Ray Hangge and duck house inventor Tom Tubbs among them. They fought back with a battle cry: "Save the Game Lakes." The result was the Minnesota Waterfowl Association, which went on to preserve wetlands in hundreds of places and stop the degradation of "game lakes." Sadly, after fifty-two years the association folded for reasons only waterfowl hunters will see when looking in a mirror.

As the years passed, I realized that local and inspired hunters and anglers, lakeshore owners, nature lovers, and so forth were the most powerful weapons to protect Minnesota's fish and wildlife, parks and trails, and wild places. And I still believe that.

I can only hope that over the decades, my words and accounts, my television shows and scripts played even a small part in maintaining or improving Minnesota's fish and wildlife resources, our outdoor getaways, and the quality of outdoor life for which Minnesotans are famous. I just wrote quite a mouthful. What I meant to say is: Lord knows, I tried.

AND SO IT BEGINS

Being a Child Again

Opening day is coming . . . and I am a child again.

Lately, my night dreams are of lakes and loon calls, sunrises and soft walleye bites. The issues of the day, I cannot follow. Yard work and peeling paint, I cannot see. Instead, my heart brims with anticipation, single purpose and undiluted.

Opening day is coming . . . and I am a child again.

No confession. No apology, either. I don't anticipate heavy fish stringers, although I will be pursuing fish. Do not misunderstand. I will set the hook if the opportunity arises. And some fish I will kill. Others caught will swim again. Call it the compassion of a grown-up, if you want. But it is more complex than that.

Opening day is coming . . . and I am a child again.

'Tis the spirit of angling that binds me, I believe. I can feel it, I think. And it is shared by others who ply the waters, I suspect. If not, why would anglers say that the fishing is always good, even if the catching was not? The fishing, ah yes.

Opening day is coming . . . and I am a child again.

Place me on open water in search of a mystery. Eternal, it is that. My last cast shall fall, my lifetime shall end, and still, still there will be unanswered questions about the deep. I hope so. For in the eternal search there is unending discovery, infatuation, surprise, intrigue.

Opening day is coming . . . and I am a child again.

And with it comes humility. It's inherent in the angling sport. I may be the superior species. The Bible says so. But fish can't read. They live as their instincts dictate. Instincts, and the forces of their watery environment. And neither is under control of even the most skilled with rod and reel. The angler may only hope to adapt, to dangle the bait in a manner acceptable to the fishes today. And wish for luck. Because tomorrow, it will be different.

Opening day is coming . . . and I am a child again.

For the essence of the angling sport has not changed. It's just as I remember. Yet my fishing toys are more expensive, sophisticated. And anglers talk differently. The "hot spot" of yesteryear is known now as a "structure." A "good day" of fishing now means you "were on a pattern." Our lures today are mostly of modern plastic, with lifelike finishes. We have electronic eyes-to-the-bottom in boxes with computers, buttons, and something called GPS. However, the catching game remains the same. The fish still has options: to open its mouth or not.

Opening day is coming . . . and I am a child again.

I can't wait. The other kids will be there too. A fine collection, they are. Good people, friendly and kind. Oh, you'll find a bum in a boat or two. Fish hogs or plain, ornery human souls. But they're rare in the fishing fraternity, unusually rare. A coincidence? I don't think so. Fisherfolk are a special breed. Who could cast a single hook overboard and do it with optimism and NOT be special? Who could visit the beautiful places on earth, listen to the wild sounds, watch the sunset, be one with it all . . . and NOT be special?

Opening day is coming . . . and I am a child again.
And I refuse to grow up. Ever.

All About Me

North is a magic direction.
And no matter where you live, there's a North.
For generations, simply the idea of going North has been enough to
Lift The Human Spirit higher than any other direction.

— Ron Schara for *Up North* by Joe Brandmeier

I've been thinking about using the following line for a long time. Can't remember who used it first; a comedian, I suspect. Nevertheless, it's a perfect opening sentence to begin a life's story.

I was born at a very young age.

Isn't that hilarious? Don't say you didn't smile at least a bit.

It all began in Postville, a small farm town in northeast Iowa, a place that looks nothing like most of Iowa. My wonderful mom was Evelyn, who grew up in Marquette, Iowa, a river town on the Mississippi. My dad, Harlan, was raised on a farm outside of Postville. He was a fine and gifted carpenter who could build anything, from dairy barns to beautiful birch kitchen cupboards.

I so wanted to follow in his footsteps. Sadly, hammers didn't do well in my hand. Bent nails; chewed wood. "I'll find something else for you to do," he'd say, taking the hammer. Later, his advice was more direct. I still can hear him: "Ronnie, don't be a carpenter; find something else to do." I did as he said, of course. Dad lived long enough to know my chosen career was to hunt and fish

Ron as a young boy modeling a famous artwork.

and write about it. He was very proud. However, I still can't build a wood box.

My mother was the epitome of kind. Since I was her firstborn, every school paper I carried home was preserved. My other five siblings—three brothers, two sisters—weren't so revered, I guess. One of those papers was an essay I wrote in fourth grade. Years later Mom showed the paper to me; my fourth grade teacher, Miss Witt, had written at the top: "Ronnie, you have the ability to write." And, well, here I am.

I have many fond memories about growing up in Postville (population 1,500), although I've been gone for more than half a century. It was small enough to bike from one end to the other; rabbits and pheasants lived along the railroad tracks east of town. A trout stream, Livingood Springs, was about six miles north. Postville was settled by mostly German Scandinavian farmers and businessmen and, by today's standards, was very white. Looking back, growing up in Postville was a blessing but a long way from the real world.

Except on Friday nights under the lights. The black and red football uniforms of the Postville Pirates would take the field. You probably already suspected I was a Pirate football star in 1960. All Upper Iowa Conference, first team. First team, Eastern Iowa All Conference selection. Right guard on offense; linebacker on defense. God, I was good. Football scholarship offers started rolling in.

And I didn't accept any. Nope. I had other hopes and dreams that didn't start in a huddle. I was gonna be another Andy Williams, the big-time crooner. Yes, I was a singer and a trumpet player in high school. Don't mean to brag, but pretty dang good at getting onstage. Made good money singing in Bob and Linda's Bar in Prairie du Chien one summer, fifteen dollars a night, three nights a week. Gas was twenty-eight cents a gallon. I was good and rich.

I also had a voice scholarship offer from MacPhail College of Music in Minneapolis. In the autumn of 1960, I loaded my 1949 Ford Coupe (earned while working a summer on a dairy farm, fifty cows milked twice a day) and headed north out of town on Highway 51.

Postville was in my rearview mirror . . . and I was forever northbound.

A BOY AND HIS MEMORIES

How It All Began

Fishing has been a part of my life for as long as I can remember. And continues despite the passing of almost all of my angling mentors. At first, fishing was always on Sunday afternoons.

My father, Harlan, worked six days a week, but on Sunday afternoons we—Mom, Dad, me, and my siblings—headed to the Mississippi River to spend the day fishing from shore. We'd catch bluegills or sheepshead or whatever would bite by using gobs of worms.

Our worms always were hand collected in empty Folgers coffee cans. On Sunday mornings, Dad and I would go behind the livestock barns. With a pitchfork, he'd turn over fertile soil while I nabbed the squirming worms. We were good at it.

However, I wasn't always the perfect fishing partner. On my dad's chin was a scar that appeared later in his life. One of his kids put that scar there with a hook and a wad of lead sinkers. That be me.

"Almost knocked me out too," Dad recalled in later years.

It happened one day while I was casting into the Mississippi River in pursuit of sheepshead. Actually, we were fishing for walleyes, but all I ever caught were ugly sheepshead. To catch one was like pulling in a wet towel. Anyway, I digress. Dad was standing on the riverbank a good twenty yards downstream. He was unaware that I was about to make a sidearm cast—one of those rear-back-and-let-her-fling types of casts—with a gob of worms and a pound of sinkers.

How was I supposed to know my cast was going sideways? The hook and sinkers whacked the side of Dad's face, ripping the skin pretty good. As I recall, Dad didn't swear much. Just a bad cast. We didn't go fishing together for weeks after that. Not until the stitches came out.

A passion for fishing has many branches on my family tree. My grandmothers and grandfathers on both sides of the family would often go fishing on Sundays. Of all my grandparents, Grandma Dickens was the best at catching. I'm not sure why. Patience, perhaps. She believed in getting a bite, I think.

My mother, Evelyn, had the same fishing genes. She could sit on the shore for hours watching the tip of her fishing rod for a bite. My dad was pretty good at fishing, but Mother held her own at the end of a fishing day.

My uncles on both sides of the family tree—Schara and Dickens—were avid anglers. Two of my mother's brothers—Uncle Ed and Uncle Bob—were fly fishermen who willingly shared the skills of fly casting for wary trout in the streams of northeast Iowa.

Those are the angling seeds planted in me as a boy, seeds that eventually sprouted.

Along the way, some of my fishing mentors have made their last casts. My mother died of cancer at age fifty-five. I still remember the day she caught more walleyes on Mille Lacs than Dad or me. Dad's last fishing trip was the 1981 Minnesota walleye opener with his sons. Then he went home to die two months later at age sixty-seven. My uncles—Ray Schara, Ken Schara, Charles Schara, Harvey Dickens, Ed Dickens, Lawrence Dickens—fishing enthusiasts who touched my life, are gone too.

I remember the day Uncle Ray took me fishing and he caught all the fish. I bawled about it. Lord knows, Uncle Ray tried to change my fishing fate. For some reason, Uncle Ray's bobber was being pulled down all the time by a fish. My bobber never moved.

Uncle Ray suggested we switch cane poles. I eagerly agreed. Now I would watch his bobber; he would watch mine. Then, Uncle Ray's bobber—which used to be my bobber—started going down, and he was pulling up bluegills and having a good old time. In a weak, sniffling voice, I demanded that we switch poles again. We did. To my amazement the bobber that just had been mine was now going down as soon as Uncle Ray was holding the cane pole.

As tears gathered in my eyes, Uncle Ray said sternly that I wasn't being patient long enough for the bluegills to find my bait. He said I had to leave my hook in the water for at least fifteen seconds if I expected my bobber to go down. But I didn't listen.

Looking back, I can't explain my lack of patience or why the bluegills liked Uncle Ray best. But we laughed about it for years. After my tears dried.

As I write this, only one of my fishing mentors is left—Uncle Bob Dickens, who was my best trout fishing instructor. Later, he became the source of many of the fishing yarns included in these pages. Uncle Bob's head is full of boastful fishing stories, some true. He also can tease with a straight face, and he honed his teasing skills on me.

In my eyes, however, Uncle Bob was a magician with a fly rod, and wily brown trout were no match for his angling skills. Plain and simple, when I was a boy, Uncle Bob was my trout fishing idol. We spent many days on trout streams, such as Waterloo Creek. Sometimes we'd camp out in a tent to be at the trout holes at first light or to catch grasshoppers for bait while the morning chill slowed their jumping escapes.

Fond memories all. But I do remember one night in the tent, just as I was about to fall asleep, Uncle Bob mumbled, "P U, smell that swamp."

As I held my nose, I believed Uncle Bob. Must be a swamp. Swamps stink. Then I remembered, what swamp?

A Special Christmas Gift

One of the joys of the Christmas season are gifts that over time become unforgettable. We've all had them. One of mine was from my father.

My present was under the Christmas tree. Guessing what was encased in the wrapping wasn't difficult. My dad watched quietly as his son began to open the long box. Perhaps the father could see himself a generation before when he held a similar package.

A boy doesn't forget his first gun. Fathers don't either. Mine was a .410 shotgun, a single-shot model. It was used, a hand-me-down bought from the local hardware store for less than fifteen dollars. That didn't matter. The tiny nicks and scratches on the walnut stock would be there sooner or later, I figured. It was a single-shot with a hammer and a top lever break-open action. At first my thumb was too weak to cock the hammer, but I learned how in a day. To my eyes, it was a beautiful sporting arm. Just the weapon I needed for those elusive cottontails that lived along the railroad tracks on the edge of town.

Only later did I learn that my father's decision to give me a shotgun was not done in haste. We had previously walked together through several hunting seasons. He had watched my gun safety manners.

In the beginning I carried nothing. Later, I held my BB gun while we hunted squirrels. Finally, my father allowed me to hunt squirrels with his single-shot .22 rifle that, oddly enough, was one of *his* memorable Christmas presents. As the autumns passed, the lessons passed from father to son. A gun is not a toy. The enjoyment of hunting is how you play the game. Be a marksman, not a shooter. Safety means everything.

Some lessons came hard. One day, returning from a rabbit hunt, I brought the .22 rifle into the house and propped it up in its usual corner. My father later checked the rifle. When he opened the chamber he found a spent .22 shell. Technically, the gun was harmless. To my father, however, the empty shell still in the chamber was evidence that I had not checked the rifle before bringing it into the house. My father placed the old rifle off-limits for a week. The lesson would last a lifetime.

On the day after Christmas, flush with my new weapon, I figured the rabbits were in trouble. In my five-buckle overshoes, I trudged toward the weed patches to confront a cottontail with my .410. Those tricky rabbits had long outmaneuvered a single-shot .22. Their zigzag dash through the thickets easily frustrated boys and marksmen as well. Now the playing field was level. Those cottontails no longer had the advantage. With a shotgun, strict accuracy was not required. With a shotgun, it would be easy to dump a streaking rabbit.

I felt superior. And the very first rabbit I spotted was sitting motionless in a clump of grass, not ten yards away. Such an easy target for a .410, I thought. Too easy. I walked toward the rabbit and kicked the grass. Like a bouncing powder puff, the cottontail streaked down the ditch. The boy waited. He fired. The rabbit kept on running. I couldn't believe my eyes. Then, I had to smile a little, although it hurt to do so. If you're gonna miss a rabbit with a .410, it might as well be your first one.

But I learned something that day. Rabbit hunting would always possess the ingredients that made me love the sport.

Today some folks think a gun is a ridiculous present to give to a teenage son or daughter. Some parents view firearms as only tools for destruction. Those views are foreign to me. I learned responsibility with a firearm and honed the skills of marksmanship with rifle or shotgun. My firearms have been along on some of my life's most memorable experiences—from the pristine wilderness of Alaska's Kodiak Island to, yes, the weedy ditches of the Rock Island Line.

Some fathers understand that. In time, some boys will too.

Going Home Again

They say there's no going home again. But how do they know? Well, I think I found the answer. It was lurking along the banks of the Yellow River and a dainty tributary of spring water known as Livingood Springs.

I used to know the Livingoods who lived near the springs. They don't live there anymore. In fact, lots of folks I used to know no longer live where I remember them. Many don't live at all.

To reach Livingood Springs, there's an old and winding stretch of highway to follow north of my hometown. Once upon a time, the road curved around a picturesque bluff called Horseshoe Bend and then snaked northeastward among rolling woodlands with fields and pastures carved out of the original oak and maple hillsides.

I remember the route well, for it was a boy's path to adventure and mischief. For me and Joe Ball. And sometimes Bobby Brouillet. We coveted our chance to explore Livingood Springs because it was a trout stream and we were thirteen-year-old trout fishing experts.

Back then, I may have been an authority on how to catch trout, although Joe usually caught the biggest ones. And Bobby tied the better flies and thus held expert status—that is, until the day he heard rattlesnakes along the banks of Livingood. As I recall, Bobby and I were crossing a strip of tall prairie alongside the stream just at dusk. *Rattle, rattle.* "Rattlesnake," I shouted, jumping back. Bobby froze, his legs not more than a foot from the last rattle. He began to quiver like a willow branch in a windstorm. Joe jumped back at the same time I did, just as we'd planned.

We knew Bobby had no time for snakes. In the dark, those flying grasshoppers sound just like a rattler's tail. We finally confessed to Bobby. He took it like a trout expert would.

Years later I looked for the piece of native prairie where we launched our plot to scare Bobby Brouillet. It was gone. Plowed to plant corn and eroded away by the stream. Gone also was the Big Pool where all the trophy trout lived. In fact, there wasn't much that hadn't changed. What was pretty wasn't pretty anymore.

Oh, the tallest limestone cliff is still there. Joe and I tried to climb it one day when the trout weren't hitting. We would have reached the top, too, if Joe, who was leading the climb, hadn't kicked out a small boulder that fell on top of my head. It nearly knocked me silly.

The place called Horseshoe Bend also changed. There was a time when the best squirrel hunter in Allamakee County once roamed the wooded hillside. That be me.

Horseshoe Bend was a dreamland with limestone walls and caves where, no doubt, mountain lions and wolves lived in a young hunter's mind. The woods also was full of smart squirrels, fox and grays. Years ago the best squirrel hunter in Allamakee County announced that when he dies his ashes were to be spread amid the towering oak and hickory trees of Horseshoe Bend. But now: a change of plans.

A big chunk of Horseshoe Bend has been modified forever. It's a stone quarry now. And much of the woods has been either logged or cleared. I don't want to be there. Indeed, there's no going back home, they say. Sometimes it's too painful to try.

Teens and Trout

It should be noted that often Minnesota's trout season opens in weather that would discourage a hungry river otter. It's an unfortunate but natural phenomenon, of course. And as such, the Department of Natural Resources and the local weather forecasters are blameless in the matter.

Season openers on indecent and inclement weekends should serve as a reminder that trout fishing can be a hairy endeavor. Parents, truant officers, outdoor writers, and other so-called experts long have preached that angling is a gentle, healthy, nonviolent pursuit. Fishing is the perfect solution, they say, for kids gone astray. Show a kid the babbling brooks and flowering meadows, and the kid will go forever straight, forsaking those devilish pranks hatched by teenagers loafing on the town street corners.

I think Joe Ball's mother believed that. And I think that is the reason she was always willing to drive Joe and me to a trout stream in the summer. She always said that a boy on a trout stream would experience the lessons of life that lead to future greatness. Casting into a trout pool, the boy would witness the wonders of nature, the rewards of his own persistence. Yet he'd also learn to accept humility in confronting a trout that ignored the boy's hooks with impunity. I'm not sure Joe Ball's mother believed all of that, but it's possible.

And so Joe Ball's mother was the first choice on Saturday mornings when it was time to find a ride out to Livingood Springs, six miles out of Postville. She was a gentle, understanding woman, proud that Joe and I were seeking the harmless environs of a stream instead of the empty cattle barns at the fairgrounds. Some kids went there to smoke and carry on.

When she agreed to give us a ride, her only requirement was that when it was time to go home she would blow the car horn and we were to promptly quit fishing and meet her on the road. One time she had to blow the horn for forty-five minutes, and she didn't like that.

Joe was the best thirteen-year-old trout fisherman I ever knew. He told me the same thing. We got along very well as long as our Saturday fishing results were about equal. For a while Joe had the edge as a fly fisherman because he caught a trout once. All I could get with an artificial black gnat were creek chubs. "Catching chubs with a fly is good practice for trout," Joe would say, coaching me and reminding me that he'd already succeeded.

My favorite trout killer was a Hildebrandt spinner, size 0, fished on a fly rod. Joe liked Colorado spinners until I outfished him with the Hildebrandt. We both specialized with night crawlers if needed.

There were days, however, when nothing worked. No matter how, where, or what we fished we could not catch a trout. We did not even see a trout.

When that happened, Joe and I turned to another sport: climbing the sheer limestone bluffs above the stream. We had the common sense not to discuss this diversion with Joe Ball's mother. She knew the bluffs were there. And she knew the rocky ledges and stunted cedars were the strict domain of birds and rattlesnakes. She did not know that Joe and I viewed the bluffs as something to conquer if the fishing turned slow.

On one particular Saturday the trout fishing was most discouraging. Neither of us had had a strike or a nibble. And we had exhausted our trout tricks. This assessment of our trout-fishing woes was reached at the base of a rather spectacular bluff that erupted at the edge of a deep pool. It was, by far, the steepest bluff along the stream and one that we had avoided lest we ruin our perfect climbing record. For no bluff had yet defeated us.

Yet the fishing was particularly miserable, a conclusion we had reached quite early in the day. Joe Ball's mother wouldn't be back to pick us up for another three hours. What were we supposed to do?

Together, we approached the limestone bluff. Joe led the expedition. It was easier than it looked. With natural footholds in the limestone and handy cedar tree roots for grasping, we quickly reached a halfway point. Golly, we were expert rock climbers as well as trout seekers. Down below, the stream's white riffles and blue-green pools glittered in the sun. The view was pretty but kinda unsettling.

Gradually, our climbing rate slowed. Another obstacle, a fat ledge, was above us. We were being tested. Joe said it might be best if I waited on a solid ledge while he attempted to find an upward path. I was content to wait, not looking up and afraid to look down.

And so I didn't see it coming. The rock was the size of a softball. It must have broken loose when Joe lifted a foot. You can't hear falling rocks until they hit something. This rock merely bounced dead center off the top of my skull and continued on down. The lights in my eyes faded briefly, then reappeared in time to verify that I was still on the ledge, despite a strong sensation of dizziness, quickly replaced by a feeling of wetness underneath my baseball cap. It was blood, the appearance of which canceled the rest of the climb. When the bleeding finally stopped, my head of hair had a caked appearance much like the back of a sow lying in a mud wallow.

Joe and I picked up our fishing rods, creels, and vests and headed for the road. His mother was honking the car horn. As I approached the car, her eyes widened. "What happened to you?"

"I got hit on the head by a rock," I replied.

She never asked why. Joe said nothing.

I said fishing was slow.

She didn't ask why. Joe said nothing.

The Blonde, the Duckling, and Me

She was a pretty blonde with a friendly smile. She was standing behind the counter of a gambling game on the midway at the Mower County Fair.

I wanted her attention, I guess, when I stepped up and reached into my pocket for money. But what I really wanted she held in her hands, the game's prize—a real live duckling, a cute fuzzy little ducky covered in yellow down.

"To win a duckling," she said, "all you have to do is pitch a nickel onto a saucer." And make it stay there. "No leaning over the counter," she ordered.

I tried it twice. Both nickels ricocheted off the saucer and landed on a canvas floor paved with other nickels. The blonde smiled at me. She liked me, I thought. I wandered on, but I knew I'd be back. Near as I could tell, the best prize at the fair was a live duckling. Plus, I was sure the pretty carnival girl liked me.

When you're eleven years old, stuffed teddy bears and knick-knacks made of plaster of paris aren't as tempting. The second best deal, I figured, was the skill crane in the glass box. Cost a dime. But if you picked the right crane, and cranked with proper timing, you could scoop a bucketful of dimes out of a tray on the far side. If you were good at it you could get your money back and then some. At worst, you might end up with a pair of baby pink dice made of foam or a small iron statue of a saddled horse.

I strolled back to the pretty blonde. She remembered me, I'm sure. She held up a duckling. It peeped lonely-like. She said that was the one I could have if I put a nickel in a saucer. The pretty blonde carnival girl noticed I had a fistful of nickels. She acted like she liked me.

Tossed the first nickel like a knuckleball, no spin. Hit the plate but didn't stay. Next tried a reverse flip, but it fell short. Maybe I could bounce a nickel from one plate to another where it might settle. Tried two of those tosses. No go.

She was rooting for me, the blonde. Groaned after every throw and shouted to the people passing by about how close I'd come to winning. A small crowd gathered as I prepared to toss yet another nickel. Made me nervous. Besides that, I was getting low on nickels, although I didn't let on, what with the pretty blonde cheering and hoping like she was.

Now I was down to two, maybe three, nickels left. I can't say for sure. But I do remember giving up hope and, worse, being afraid of disappointing the pretty blonde. I flicked another nickel. It hit the plate, bounced, spun, and clattered noisily . . . on another plate. I did it! I *did* it!

The pretty blonde smiled, opened a small paper sack, and dropped the duckling inside.

"Who's next?" she shouted, holding high another duckling. It was the last time I ever saw her.

My folks didn't smile much when I showed them what I'd won. Only once was I allowed to let the duckling swim in the kitchen sink. But the duckling soon won them over. As the weeks passed, it slowly blossomed into a magnificent bird, a big white duck.

The duck was tame too. Loved to eat the grasshoppers I'd collect in one of Mom's mason quart jars. It would stick its head completely in the jar and start smacking its flat lips. Whenever Dad dug potatoes or otherwise turned over the garden soil, the bird waddled at his heels, picking up worms, grubs, bugs.

By fall my duck was full grown, of course. Unfortunately, some of the duck's habits also had increased in size, especially on the sidewalk between the garage and the house. My dad wasn't happy. It became very treacherous to walk without watching your step and tracking duck poop onto the kitchen floor. Mother didn't like it much either, and my sister had to stop running barefoot around the yard.

To help ease the tension, I volunteered to hose off the sidewalk. Sometimes I'd forget, though. When that happened, Dad renewed his threat to butcher my pet. I didn't believe him.

I don't remember exactly what set Dad off. I wasn't home at the time. But I think he stepped into a fresh pile of duck doo-doo one day and didn't know it until he saw his tracks across the kitchen floor.

So ends my lucky duck story. Today when I go to the Minnesota State Fair or the Anoka County Fair, I'm sometimes reminded of my most successful day ever on the midway. I always find that kind of sad. Brings back memories of my duck.

Firecrackers and Fishing

My childhood memories about the Fourth of July are more about fishing than firecrackers.

Unless there was a parade to watch in my hometown, my mom, my dad, and the kids—my five younger siblings and me—headed to the Mississippi River, most often in the vicinity of Marquette, Iowa, where Grandpa Clate and Grandma Blanche Dickens lived. Sometimes we drove to new fishing hot spots near Iowa river towns, such as New Albin, Harpers Ferry, or Lansing, and found our way to the river through tall nettles that guarded shore fishing spots.

My father, being a natural worrywart, wasn't into firecrackers for fear one of us kids would blow off a finger. He was almost right. In my teenage years and without my parents knowing, I think I held but one cherry bomb. Even at that, my folks found out about it. Let me explain.

My buddy Dennis Eder, a tall redheaded kid with a penchant for trouble, invited me to explore the town's stockyards as a preliminary to any July Fourth festivities. He had an idea and a stash of powerful cherry bombs. Did you know you can light a cherry bomb and toss it in water and it'll still explode? Cool stuff.

Dennis thought we would find an ideal place to watch a cherry bomb explosion behind the stockyards. And we did. It was a muddy hole filled with plenty of hog and cow manure. And since we were on the tin roof (don't ask me how) of the cattle pens, we could drop the cherry bomb with impunity and not worry about any fallout. That was the plan when the only cherry bomb I ever lit in my hand was quickly tossed into the manure-rich mudhole.

At the time, I thought my being on the roof was a safe retreat away from anything falling from the explosion of manure. I really did. Later, I realized I had underestimated the power of cherry bombs. As soon as I walked back into my house, my mother's nose was livid. This "experiment" further reduced my chances of ever, ever playing with fireworks again. Probably a good thing. I still have my fingers.

Absent firecrackers, our family July Fourth celebrations were largely spent sitting on the riverbank and lazily watching the

Mississippi roll by. We never fished from a boat because my father was convinced one of us would fall overboard.

Looking back, my dad was pretty smart. A boat is no place for children with short attention spans. On the shore we were free to create our own entertainment if the fishing was slow. Being the oldest sibling, I could always entertain myself by making Robert, my little brother, start bawling. He'd believe just about everything I'd tell him. I'd shout warnings about lions and rattlesnakes coming up right behind us. It was fun.

The Mississippi was always good for a smorgasbord of catches when using night crawlers for bait: walleyes, sheepshead, bullheads, channel cats, carp, redhorse suckers, carpsuckers, silver bass, sauger, and something my dad called "mudcats." The best fishing spots were places along the river where the current was still and bluegills lurked in the flooded brush. When the bluegills were biting, I even quit lying to Robert. Watching a bobber go down was more fun.

Yes, the July Fourths of my youth were uncomplicated holidays. Things were cane pole simple. All you had to do was watch a bobber. Today kids seem to spend more time with firecrackers. Better they go fishing on July Fourth, my dad would say. Now I say it too.

Sandbars, Bugs, and Cigarettes

It's probably safe to tell these river fishing stories now.

My boyhood fishing buddy, Don, moved away years ago and is involved, I'm told, in a respectable business somewhere out west. And my old high school, the place I used to swap for a day of river fishing, was torn down a while back. Also gone is Old Stern Face, the meanest principal I've ever known.

Actually, Old Stern Face just looked mean. Underneath those facial warts and such, I figured he was a softie and actually liked Don and me because we went fishing instead of cruising main street. I'm told he has mellowed some over the years. After I graduated, they say, Old Stern Face took up a hankering for fishing. Digs his own worms now and spits on his hook, I'm told.

If only Old Stern Face had seen the light early on, my high school days would have been much easier. Why, we could've skipped out early together to hit the river. Instead, I had to waste valuable fishing time in his office, where he did most of the talking. I once tried to convince that stuffed shirt that a day of river fishing was just as important to a young man's career as a day of classes. I suspect he agrees with me now. And I know why.

The river won him over, I'll bet. Yes, the Great River—and there's only one—the Mississippi.

I grew up where the borders of Iowa, Minnesota, and Wisconsin meet. If you said you were "on the River," your meaning was clear. Oh, there were other rivers nearby: the Yellow, the Turkey, the Upper Iowa. But if you spent a day exploring their banks and bends, you called them by name. They were rivers, yes, but mere trickles by comparison. When those rivers emptied into the River, they were no more. Done and gone, just like that. The River just kept rolling along, like the song says.

Where the River first cuts between Iowa and Wisconsin, forested hills and towering limestone bluffs stand on opposite banks as though the two states are about to rub hairy shoulders. Such rugged terrain and scenic beauty are commonplace on that stretch of the River, extending as far upstream as Red Wing, Minnesota. It's no open-water chute there. Rather, the River is a winding, watery maze—a network of backwater trails and cuts that flow amid countless islands, where the stinging nettles seem to grow almost as tall as the bottomland cottonwoods.

Historians say the River was both revered and feared by Native Americans who roamed the valley. When embarking on canoe trips, it's said, Dakota Indian leaders would say prayers and offer tobacco to the River, a ceremonial gesture to ensure a safe trip.

Don and I used to do the same thing, sort of. Only we smoked the tobacco first and then prayed we didn't get caught. Don had a knack for swiping cigarettes from his older sister. She couldn't count, I guess. Of course, we never had enough smokes to offer just for ceremony. I got all the matches wet one time, and that was bad enough.

It was the kind of place where a boy could stretch his limitations, taste the thrill of adventure, and ponder where all the water kept coming from. On the River, you didn't ever have to grow up.

My grandpa Clate Dickens was a river rat, and he never matured. Held odd jobs around Marquette, a small town on the other end of the bridge from Prairie du Chien, Wisconsin. When there wasn't much to do, Grandpa Clate and Grandma Blanche would head upstream to where the Yellow River emptied into the Mississippi. It was a natural fish attractor, and there were rocky wing dams in the River's main channel, where walleyes and sheepshead lurked.

Grandma loved to sit on the bank, plunk a gob of night crawlers into the River, and watch her rod tip for the hint of a nibble. A universal bait, night crawlers are. Apt to catch anything and often did. For Grandma, anyway. She never minded being called a fisherman. In fact, Grandma always said she was a better fisherman than Grandpa. And actually, she was.

Those were the days. Indeed, a sense of early American history lingers over the upper valley of the Mississippi. Its banks are settled by historic river towns such as Marquette, Iowa, named after the famed river explorer who once stepped ashore there, and Victory, Wisconsin, named in celebration of a battle with Black Hawk.

What the native peoples and early explorers missed, Don and I discovered, I'm sure. We would camp on the River's giant sandbars and sleep in pea-green Boy Scout sleeping bags. Don always pondered aloud whether some famous explorer or Native American leader had shared our resting place. It was a question we never stayed awake long enough to answer, drifting off to the steady hum of the River and a chorus of frogs.

Sometimes the hum was from mosquitoes. A campsite amid the River's sandbar willows might look wilderness-like, but it's no place for warm-blooded creatures beyond the hour of sundown. Better to pitch the tent out in the open, where the breezes can blow the blood vultures away from camp.

The time Don and I chose to sleep back amid the sandbar willows, we were planning to spend the night in a pup tent borrowed from his uncle, who was in World War II. It didn't have many holes. I remember it well because we were up most of the night swatting at the humming noises. Couldn't see the mosquitoes; just heard 'em. We were defenseless in the tent. No bug spray and no smoke. Come dawn, we awoke surprised to be alive.

The River is an angler's paradise, a piscatorial smorgasbord, harboring every variety a fishing enthusiast wants and a few not wanted. One day Don and I caught nine different species with the same bait, night crawlers. We had two kinds of suckers, a channel catfish, and a yellow bullhead. A largemouth bass and a sauger might have been the best of the lot. We had a couple of crappies and a few bluegills too. The ninth species was sheepshead, as I recall, not much to brag about.

I remember my father wasn't impressed. When he went to the River, it was for walleyes. He loved catching walleyes, particularly at night above the wing dams. Sometimes he caught channel catfish instead. Lots of big cats, flathead and channel. Scuba divers, I'm told, claim the River holds catfish large enough to swallow a minnow bucket. Ain't never caught such a cat or a bait bucket, but I believe it. Had one on the end of the line once, I think. It got off. Or it could have been a giant river sturgeon or a paddlefish, maybe. Those two reach weights of a hundred pounds or more.

When I was a kid, the River's banks were settled only by impoverished folks and vagabonds, living in shacks on high stilts to survive the spring floods. People with jobs and money lived away from the River, in houses built on the ground. In the last fifty years, they have switched places. Now it's the wealthy who live by the River in houses built on stilts.

Change is as normal as mayflies on the River, of course. Its powerful current, that relentless force of give and take, assures that nothing lasts forever or stays the same. And its beauty and mystique somehow survive the steady abuses brought by man and nature. There still are fish to catch and frogs to sing. Migrating fowl continue to follow its watery path and seek refuge in that vast Upper Mississippi National Wildlife and Fish Refuge. And there remains a maze of backwaters to offer solitude and adventure. That's the River of my youth. And it's still there.

Only the boy is gone.

MOTHER NATURE AND ME

Return to Livingood Springs

I went back to a boyhood trout stream not long ago. It's a place known as Livingood Springs, a short stretch of flowing water north of my hometown, named for the folks who settled along its headwaters decades ago. They say there's no going back to boyhood haunts. Maybe I should have stayed away. But I didn't, and I'm sadder for it.

One day I had heard tell that Livingood Springs—so named for a fountain of cold spring water gurgling (for centuries, probably) from a hole at the base of a limestone bluff—was dangerously low or simply had quit spewing water. Was my boyhood fishing hole a victim of nature's drought or man's destruction of natural waterways, such as sinkholes?

I felt the need to visit Livingood, as if an old friend were in trouble. I also figured my boyhood chums, Bobby Brouillet and Joe Ball, would appreciate knowing if Livingood was dead or dying. Livingood was our hangout in the worry-free summers of our youth. It was a place where boys could catch fish, climb bluffs, rip clothes, dunk shoes, and otherwise collect a layer of grime. The place was special to me, the birthplace of a lot of memories: first trout, first fly rod, first fish on an artificial lure. It's where Bobby learned about tying trout flies and concocting trout catching patterns. It's where Joe and I camped under a leaky army surplus tent, cooked on Boy Scout kits, and made meals out of the stream's rich beds of watercress.

But that's history.

Imagine my apprehension as I began the hike from Livingood's old farmstead to the spring headwaters flowing out of the wall of limestone. Although I had not been there for more than three decades, my memories of Livingood still seemed as rich as Iowa's soil. Yet I was told the spring might be dry. I quickened my footsteps. Suddenly, from a distance of several hundred yards, I thought I could hear water bubbling out of the limestone. A good sound. *Hallelujah!* Livingood wasn't dry after all. Low, but still flowing. Indeed, the rumors had been wrong, I told myself.

Then I reached the headwaters and could see for myself. Livingood wasn't dead. But it looked deathly. And I couldn't believe my eyes. When I was twelve years old, Livingood Springs consisted of trout pools and riffles of blue water with trout hideouts built by Civilian Conservation Corps (CCC) workers. It was a stream worth preserving for the next generation.

Today we're passing on to the next generation: Six rusting car bodies. Hoods and fenders in the riffles. Silted pools. Overgrazed banks. Cleared timber. And blue-gray water. Instead of a stream for trout, Livingood had become a stream of abuse, neglect, and, worse, indifference.

How could it happen, I wondered. An Iowa fisheries official told me because the stream flows through private land the state was powerless to remove the car bodies. "That's stupid," I said. The official agreed. Iowa law prohibited the Department of Natural Resources from spending money to clean up a stream that flowed through private land. Nobody else stepped up either. As I questioned Iowa officials, it became clear that Iowa's water pollution laws were weak. Upward of eight Iowa trout streams had been lost due to neglect, the officials said.

The irony?

Decades ago, government agencies, such as the CCC, spent public funds to improve Iowa's streams, private or public. Now government stands aside with weak laws and short-sighted environmental objectives. But wait: Where are the local anglers, who should be protesting such neglect of pristine water? Where are community and farm leaders, who remain silent about streams filled with trashed car bodies?

I also wondered: Does anybody in my hometown care? Who had the right to turn Livingood Springs, a trout brook, into a junk stream? When is it right to overgraze riverbanks, causing tons of silt to ruin the public's water? What is the public's right to responsible land stewardship adjoining public water?

There are no suitable answers to these questions. Besides, it's too late to save Livingood Springs. The last time I checked Iowa's DNR website, the list of state trout waters no longer included the name.

Doesn't matter.

Watercress no longer grows in the stream, eliminated by herbicide runoff, no doubt. We used to have school picnics at the headwaters. Couldn't now. No place to sit. Too much cow crap. The deep pool where Mr. Smith, the school principal, jumped into the water to land a giant brown trout? It's gone. Also gone is the junction pool where Livingood joins the Yellow River. The bridge pool? Yeah, it's gone, too.

For old time's sake, I made a cast into the first trout hole downstream from where the spring flows out from the base of the limestone bluff. It was a special place to me, the place where I caught my very first brook trout decades ago. This time there was no trout to catch. My spinner flicked alongside the right rear fender of a car body. I hope somebody someday will tell the next generation: Livingood wasn't always a junkyard.

The Pain of Gordon's Woods

Author's Note: As I looked back at my stories of old, I found several yarns about my memories of Gordon's Woods. Maybe too many. Please forgive me. Clearly, my days in Gordon's Woods were largely pleasant but, in the end, very painful. Gordon's Woods was forever changed by unrelenting chain saws and logging trucks.

Coincidentally, the man who owned Gordon's Woods was also a man for whom I worked. When I discovered the destruction of Gordon's Woods, I confronted my boss, who casually said he'd cut down the trees in hopes that someday he'd have a cornfield. I angrily told him he'd never live long enough to see cornstalks growing where Gordon's Woods once stood.

My boss was a good man. But my prediction turned out to be the right one.

It was known as Gordon's Woods, although I cannot explain why. It was the name my dad always used, which was good enough for me. Can't recall if he ever said who Gordon was.

Doesn't really matter now.

Gordon's Woods wasn't anything special, no virgin tree trunks or ecological treasure. Neither was Gordon's a large expanse of timber, probably less than a hundred acres. If Gordon's was unique, it was for other reasons, admittedly personal: Dad and I on many Sunday mornings shared a stump in Gordon's Woods to hunt squirrels. Over the years those mornings have been remembered with a special fondness. Memories, of course, tend to go off-balance with time. Maybe the mornings on the stumps were not all eventful father-son dialogues, but I've forgotten those that weren't.

I do remember it was in Gordon's Woods where a nervous kid of twelve (maybe thirteen) bagged his first squirrel. It was a gray squirrel. Killed it with a single-shot .22—a Stevens Favorite, Model 1915. It was my dad's .22 when he was a boy. My first squirrel turns out to be a special memory, although it wasn't the first squirrel in my rifle sights. All of those squirrel shots before were misses.

Doesn't really matter now. Dad is gone, dead and buried. And Gordon's Woods is gone, its carcass bulldozed into piles of twisted logs and limbs. Gordon's Woods is being turned into a cornfield. I don't know if the world needs another cornfield, but such questions are seldom asked. My immediate response to the planned cornfield was anger. Just what Iowa needs: another monotonous field of cornstalks all in a row.

But it doesn't matter now.

Perhaps the farmer who owned Gordon's Woods simply wanted another cornfield more than he wanted the woods. And who am I to judge the man on the tractor? He paid the taxes on Gordon's Woods, not I. He is in the business of raising crops, not squirrels. So what if he already had more cornland than most of his neighbors? Is it fair to say he's greedy for adding Gordon's Woods to his plowing inventory?

No, there must be other reasons why Gordon's Woods had to die. Maybe it's us. You, me, and them. Maybe it's the society we've created that wastes and splurges, that demands cheap food in expensive packages. Maybe it's we, the government, who via free spending, inflation, and trade deficits have unleashed the corn planters without weighing the consequences.

But it doesn't matter now.

There were no congressional hearings, no Sierra Club protests when the bulldozers arrived at Gordon's Woods. Only the nationally important places receive those defenses. Gordon's Woods wasn't in that category. It was just there, reached by driving out of town on the Old Creamery Road, where it survived for centuries until it was decided cornstalks were more important than walnut trees.

Maybe it means that we—you, I, and them—still haven't learned to live with a conservation conscience and to have balance—some corn, some trees. Aldo Leopold, the father of wildlife management, said we have to learn to live in harmony with the land. Sadly, we're not doing very well at following Leopold's sensible advice. We continue unharnessed and uncontrolled while another place of harmony dies.

It hurts to say, but the evidence shows the woods is gone because we killed it.

Learning a Lot Sitting in a Tree

When October comes, a fella can learn a lot sitting in a tree.

When I tree-sit I also carry a bow and arrow and my body is wrapped in enough camouflage for the entire Fifth Army. Sometimes I question why I dress in hopes deer won't see me. Those crafty whitetails seldom come my way. And when they do, my stomach leaps into my throat and my right leg goes into the darnedest quiver. The bow shakes, the arrow shakes, and I shake, as do the nearby branches.

Frankly, it's disgusting to choke up at such times. You've already spent more time in that oak than an acorn, just waiting for a deer. And now the deer is standing there, and you're quaking like an aspen. Some folks refer to this condition as "buck fever." Veteran hunters aren't supposed to get it. Well, that's a bunch of hooey. I come down with symptoms when a whitetail wanders along the trail, walking like a ghost. Bingo. Doesn't even have to be a buck.

A deer coming your way is, well, nerve-racking. I've never figured out how a deer can step on dry leaves so quietly. A man walking on the same terrain would sound like the Rock Island Line.

Now there are some things I don't enjoy when the deer is within spitting distance. (For one, I don't actually know the distance for certain because my mouth is too dry to spit.) I don't particularly enjoy hearing my own heartbeat above the rattle of two knees. Yet I think it's important that some part of me goes to pieces. If those symptoms ever cease, perhaps I should stop deer hunting. The challenge of outwitting a whitetail should always be worth a dry mouth and a few butterflies.

I must admit: years ago my buck fever symptoms were actually worse. The first time I saw a wild buck deer my legs just quit working. I had to sit down. It's not that bad anymore. Now I sit first.

When you hunt with a rifle, buck fever doesn't get as intense. I don't know why exactly. Maybe it's because a rifle gives you more range, more power. With a bow, a fella doesn't stand so tall. The biggest buck in Iowa would have been mine, except arrows don't go where bullets can. My arrow bounced off the massive set of antlers this Iowa monster had on his head. I think that ol' boy is still running from the clatter.

More deer than I can remember have passed by my tree stand untouched. A few were missed. Okay, more than a few. Others simply walked behind bushes and trees unaware of their luck.

Deer or no deer, my perch in a tree for so many Octobers has offered quite a show. I've seen and admired a whitetail's stealth. Anyone who says that deer don't wise up until hunting season opens just doesn't know. A whitetail is wise all the time. I've seen deer fight, play, breed, and die. Whitetail-watching is one of the greatest shows on earth. And it is free.

If the deer fail to appear, there's another show happening in October. Autumn begins to die before your eyes. It's always a little sad, although you've seen this show before and you knew it was coming. The signs are subtle. A leaf makes its last flicker to the wind and falls. Colorful trees reluctantly shed their golden crowns and eventually become stark, naked skeletons. Once-tall grasses bow flat, withering to an ugly brown.

Yet signs of life continue around your tree. Chipmunks squeal and squirrels bark from nearby stumps. However, as the day comes to an end and the light begins to fade, the nut-collectors act nervous. They seem to know, or at least act like they know, sunset starts a new game of survival. Down in the hollow comes the eerie call of a barred owl. It's time again to hunt on silent wings. Only the foolish squirrel lingers in the leaves or on the stump as darkness comes. It's likely that one won't see the light of day. You'd think every squirrel in the woods would know that by now. I guess you can't fix stupid—even in squirrels.

Tiny birds—juncos, chickadees, and others—share your tree for short moments, but they seem anxious to move on. Some are headed south; some are going to roost, and there's no time to linger.

Below my tree, the woodland floor starts to come alive. Small rodents, white deer mice and others, rattle the leafy carpet seeking what I do not know. They seem too dumb to mind the owl. Perhaps that's good.

Other things below the tree also seem to move, but really they don't. I've never seen a bush walk, but my mind has said it did. I guess my mind wanted to see a whitetail on the trail. For a second the bush would do.

Finally, the time has come to climb down from my tree. The show is over—at least, the show I can still see. On this October day, there is no hunting tale to tell, no elusive whitetail to whine about. But I'm not disappointed.

A fella can learn a lot sitting in a tree.

The Br'er Fox of Horseshoe Bend

"Nothing's perfect," sighed the fox. "My life is monotonous. I hunt chickens; people hunt me. All chickens are just alike, and all men are just alike. So I'm rather bored."

—Antoine de Saint-Exupéry, *The Little Prince*

North of my hometown of Postville, Iowa, there's a long, wooded ridge with small clearings amid the oak/basswood stands, with caves in the limestone bluffs and red foxes in the thickets. The place is called Horseshoe Bend, and I spent many Thanksgiving school vacations there, especially after I learned to drive the family's 1951 Ford.

When I drove to Horseshoe Bend, I carried an old single-shot .22 rifle and high hopes to shoot a fox, something I'd never accomplished. Frankly, this confrontation—between fox and me—had to happen. Squirrel and rabbit hunting I had already mastered. If I was going to become the greatest hunter in Allamakee County, sooner or later I'd have to claim the hide of a red fox and be honest about it.

It wouldn't be easy, I knew. Despite countless forays into Horseshoe Bend for squirrels and rabbits, I'd never crossed paths with a real live fox. Only the tracks, quarter-sized dots in the snow that went single file as if made on a pogo stick. A farm dog usually left larger paw prints and walked differently, leaving a double row of marks in the snow. Well, sort of. But there was no mistaking the two.

It snowed hard on Thanksgiving Day the year I learned to drive the family Ford. Perfect conditions, I thought. My uncle Harvey, who probably was the best fox hunter in Clayton County, often told of how he'd cross a fresh fox trail after a snow and follow it until he walked the animal down or pushed it into a den. Nothing to it, he'd said. Eventually you'd get a shot because a fox will get curious about who's following. Sounded almost too easy.

I'd heard of other hunting methods to nail a red fox. Circle hunts used to be popular. A whole bunch of hunters would gather Sunday afternoons, surround a farm section, and march toward the middle, eventually reducing a fox's escape routes. But on circle hunts everybody took credit if a fox was killed. That technique was no way to become the greatest hunter in Allamakee County. Nope, the fox and I would go at it one-on-one.

On the day after Thanksgiving I struck out early. The snow had quit sometime in the night, which meant that every fox track would be fresh. I hadn't walked but fifty yards into Horseshoe Bend when, sure enough, there was a set of tracks crossing an old logging road. I started to follow. Didn't matter where the tracks led me because I knew every inch of Horseshoe Bend except where the prickly ash grew.

Prickly ash is a short tree with needlelike thorns that reach out and stab anything taller than thirty-six inches that walks upright. The only way out of prickly ash is to follow your own blood trail.

The fox I was tailing ambled into a shallow draw, walked on a few fallen logs in tightrope fashion, and eventually moseyed back up the ridge. Judging by its tracks, I figured the fox had no purpose in mind and didn't have a clue who was following. The fox trail continued southward to the edge of the timber to a large pasture with a dry creek, slough grass, and a few wild plum thickets. A farmhouse could be seen on a distant hill. The fresh tracks headed for the pasture. I followed, watching the grassy hillsides ahead and the creek bottom for any sign of red fur.

Can't say exactly when the fox first spotted me. But when I saw the fox it was leaving a trail of snow dust and zigzagging like a mouse in a maze. I raised my single-shot .22, but then thought better. As Uncle Harvey always said, "Just walk 'em down."

I continued after the fox, which was now leaving a galloping trail that consisted of marks in the snow six feet apart. An hour later I found myself walking within thirty yards of the farmhouse, exactly the path the fox took in broad daylight. The farmer wasn't home.

I also learned that trailing a running fox is a depressing experience. The ground a fox covers in one minute might take you thirty. Uncle Harvey never mentioned that. By now I was sweating a bunch. Had my coat open and had removed my mittens long ago. My legs were starting to feel a little mushy too.

After passing the farmhouse, the fox managed to circle back toward Horseshoe Bend, the wooded ridge. The tracks led through a pasture draw with a timbered cliff at the end. Steadily I lumbered on. The story in the snow told me the fox was walking again.

At the base of the cliff, the fox tracks climbed upward. I followed, slipping and sliding and panting up the cliff. At the top, the tracks stopped, replaced by a small, round spot of melted snow. I knew immediately what had happened. That damned fox had been sitting at the top of the cliff watching me walk up the draw. When the fox figured I was getting too close, it merely turned and trotted straight into the largest prickly ash patch in all of Horseshoe Bend.

Well, no fox was going to trick me. I wasn't about to enter any patch of prickly ash. Been there; done that. I quit the fox trail right then and there, ending another Thanksgiving vacation.

I've been thankful ever since.

Why We Love Antlers

In all things of nature there is something of the marvelous.

—Aristotle

A scientist might describe antlers as merely calcium deposits atop the skull of a deer. And that they are. A deer hunter might describe antlers as, well, awesome. However, nothing really explains our long fascination with antlers in any form—antlers on living heads, antlers on dead heads, antlers shed on the ground, antlers stuck in giant tractor tires.

All of us—hunters and nonhunters alike—will pause at the sight of antlers. Some people collect antlers; a growing number of folks hunt for shed antlers as if the dropped tines were as tasty as morel mushrooms. Even your hunting dog can be trained to sniff out sheds, inspiring antler zealots to hold shed-finding contests for dogs of any ilk.

Some sets of antlers are so coveted they've been stolen. Why? Usually because they are of record size and, remember, no sets of antlers are ever alike. Seems our fascination with antlers knows no end. We and antlers go back a long time. Antlers were drawn on cave walls ages ago, and now they hang on the walls of fancy homes.

Of all the wonders that grow on earth, one of them certainly is antlers. Antlers grow on deer. On elk. On moose. On caribou. And grow anew once a year, never the same look twice. That's right: unlike horns—which are totally different body parts—a new set of antlers grows every year starting in late spring. A thin, fragile, velvet-like skin, rich in blood vessels, deposits bone-like calcium and—presto—antlers. Horns, found on cattle, wild sheep, pronghorns, buffalo, even rhinos, consist of modified hair. A horn is never shed (although pronghorns shed the outer layer).

Truth be told, antlers are all about sex appeal. Come fall, the antlers on deer, elk, moose, and caribou are simply symbols of male libido—a crown if you will, to impress females and intimidate male rivals. Antlers are a male thing—except for caribou cows. Yes, cow caribou have antlers. Go figure.

Although you can't tell an animal's age by counting the points on an antler, males in their prime tend to sport the largest sets. Trophy-sized antlers require time. A buck whitetail needs five or more years to develop an exceptional rack. A bull elk needs ten years to reach its antler peak.

Our fascination with antlers has not yet found its end. We keep books of record antlers. We hang antlers in odd configurations, such as lamps and chandeliers. We use antlers for table legs. Antlers even inspire poetry in some of us. Okay, maybe just me.

Antlers, oh antlers.
You grow so divine.

Yet mystery surrounds
every antler design.

Like when do they branch
or grow a new tine?

If men were like male deer
in the rut in the fall
we'd all want big antlers
to make us look tall.

Be careful what you wish for
when you answer such a call.
Or your head and your antlers
may hang on somebody's wall.

For the Love of Chickadees

Love is being in the company of chickadees. You probably already knew that. Minnesota is an all-season home to the black-capped chickadee, a smidgen of a bird that defies Minnesota's coldest winters and meanest Aprils.

Chickadees have a huge range of admirers, from little old ladies in tennis shoes to unshaven deer hunters in blaze orange. At the sight of a chickadee, this diverse bunch will melt into a mutual admiration society for the bird's dapper dress and nonpartisan friendliness. It'll visit your backyard bird feeder or sit on your rifle barrel in the deer woods. Nature writer Tom Brown once observed that while we may learn patience from an owl or cleverness from a crow or courage from a blue jay, it's the chickadee we admire most of all for its indomitable spirit.

Not that all is hunky-dory in a chickadee's life. A chickadee rarely lives more than thirty months. Winter is the most common grim reaper. On those winter days when the temperature sinks below zero, it's difficult to understand how any bird weighing less than a handful of paper clips can thrive. But it does, thanks to an amazing winter survival system.

Chickadees are prepared. They stash food tidbits, seeds and such, and months later exhibit a remarkable ability to recall where. Studies of the chickadee's brain have shown that the memory part, the hippocampus, expands in autumn and contracts in spring, when a good memory is less critical to survival. When the days and nights cool, a chickadee will begin shivering its chest muscles to generate heat. A chickadee's feathers, when fluffed for insulation, are a homeowner's dream. Bird expert George Harrison noted that in cold weather the bird's feathers puff up to create an inch-thick coat. It might be below zero an inch outside those feathers, but the temperature of the chickadee's body core will be more than a hundred degrees. Chickadees also eat a lot. Roughly ten percent of their body weight must be consumed every day to be burned at night for energy. To conserve energy overnight, chickadees roost in cavities or deep into evergreen boughs and turn down their thermostats.

While the bird's normal body temperature is 108 degrees during the day, its body temp drops to ninety degrees on the evening roost.

By now we're all thinking, "The poor things, we must fill the bird feeders to save 'em." Not really. A Wisconsin study about the bird's rate of winter survival revealed that chickadees that did not have our bird feeders survived as well as those that flew to our human handouts. However, there was one big exception. When winter temps dropped below ten degrees, chickadees that had access to black sunflower seeds, the best option in feeders, almost doubled their survival rate compared to those that did not receive the supplemental handouts.

It's probably safe to say that, while we all admire the chickadee, there are few among us who'd like to live like one. Yet there would be advantages. We could pig out and not gain any weight. Friends would offer compliments. *How do you stay so thin over the holidays? Sunflowers? Are they flavored? You can't weigh much more than a few paper clips.*

There's one more reason to keep chickadees on our most-admired list. In late February, you may hear the chickadee sing *fee-bee, fee-bee*, the bird's call for courtship.

Yah, in February, no less. Just in time for Valentine's Day. The little twerp.

Wrens: Birds of Song

Of all the birds that sing, the most melodic song—loud and clear, a wonderous arpeggios—is performed by a bird with a tiny beak on tiny wings and tiny legs.

Therein, perhaps, flies a lesson for us all.
It's the size of the message when the messenger isn't tall.
When you're sad and lonely or life isn't what it should be.
Take a walk in the morning in the bird's company.
Listen from the heart while it sings you its song.
Tweet, tweetle, dee, tweetle dee—and your troubles will be gone.

—(writer unknown, but could be me?)

Wrens long have amused us. Such a small bird with such a loud voice. As a result, we like to concoct wild wren lore:

One day the birds were determining the "king of birds" by seeing who could fly the highest. The bald eagle flew to the sun and proclaimed victory—until a wren jumped out of the eagle's feathers and flew higher to claim the title.

The house wren is the only wren I know, although some fifty wren species fly about. While its small size is well noted, wrens are not the smallest in the bird world: kinglets and hummingbirds are smaller. The life expectancy of wrens is about four years, although most don't reach age three and only a fourth survive to age two. It's not easy to be a wren out there in the real world.

To seek the company of wrens, many of us hang wren houses. Wrens typically nest in cavities, hence their scientific name *Troglodytes aedon*, which means "little cave dweller."

When you watch a pair of wrens it becomes apparent males and females are identical in appearance. It's a good thing the wrens know who's who. However, if you see a wren singing, it is the male because females keep their mouth shut, only chirping softly. Nor is the male bashful or prone to stage fright. It may belt out a song as often as a thousand times an hour, tweeting twenty to thirty notes with five renditions and thirty versions.

In the spring—late April or early May—male wrens reach Minnesota ahead of females by ten days to two weeks. On arrival, the male wren quickly hauls twigs and sticks to a number of potential nesting sites (usually three to four), such as wren houses, tree cavities, and so forth. When a female arrives, the male leads her to his prepared nesting sites. She may reject the choices or fly on in search of a different mate with better real estate. Once satisfied with a summer home site, she may start lining one of the nests with grass and feathers. If so, it's a match.

After mating, the female wren lays seven dime-sized eggs that are cream colored with rusty swirls. Only the female incubates the eggs. Two weeks later, the eggs hatch. Newly hatched wrens are featherless and about three-quarters of an inch high. The male usually helps feed the young, who grow quickly, leaving the nest in about two weeks.

However, the wren pair are not empty nesters for long. A second brood may be on their minds, but a strange phenomenon may take place: the male or female may decide to seek a new mate. A divorce wren-style. Mate switching after the first brood is fledged is common about fifty percent of the time, studies show. The second brood typically numbers only four young.

Soon after, our midwestern days get shorter and cooler. Starting in September, Minnesota-based wrens head south, mainly to Texas and Louisiana. It's a long haul on a six-inch wing span, fifteen hundred miles one way. Unlike waterfowl, robins, and other species that migrate in flocks, the wren hits the road on a solo flight, flying day or night.

If anything, the wrens in our backyards offer another lesson in life: some mighty big accomplishments can be found in small packages. Said William Blake, "No bird soars too high if he soars with his own wings."

HUNTING AND CONSERVATION

A Confession to Hunter Haters

Most hunters prepare for the hunting season. I brace for it.

If autumn means opening day on small and big game for hunters, it also means opening day on me for anti-hunters. I'm the target, especially in autumn when I write about hunting and its worth. My critics employ letters (signed and unsigned) or email, and most lectures go like this: ridiculed first, scolded next, and then told to "drop dead." This setup often takes two to three pages written in longhand. If the lecture arrives on a postcard, there's less room for chitchat of course. The writer goes straight to the point and suggests where I ought to stick my shotgun. I seldom take the advice, but there's no escaping it.

Am I guilty of something? No, I did not crawl up on Farmer Jones's pond and spray birdshot on his pet ducks. I would never do that without asking permission. Simply, my crime is being a hunter and writing stories about hunting. Specifically, I'm accused of glamorizing a barbaric sport, promoting cruelty to animals, and, generally, acting uncivilized.

I have decided to respond to those charges with the following stipulations:

I will describe the smell and sight of gutting a deer when Hormel advertises its boneless hams by showing how the pig was killed.

I will admit that hunting causes some animal suffering if my critics will agree that hunting also eliminates some animal suffering.

As for acting uncivilized: If that means rising before dawn, dressing in camo, and talking at 4 AM about the morning's duck hunt with Coot, the black Lab, then I am guilty.

If it means watching a sunrise ooze into a forest on opening day of deer season, then count me guilty.

If it means sneaking and stalking, watching and listening, studying and admiring the wild creature I'm hunting, then I am guilty.

If it's uncivilized to buy a hunting license to kill, a license which is used also to protect, to preserve, to replenish wildlife, then I am guilty.

If it's uncivilized to think of wildlife as renewable resources to be used wisely for our own benefits, then I am more than guilty.

If it's uncivilized to donate money to buy habitat to raise more wildlife, including game and nongame species, then my guilty verdict is absolute.

If being uncivilized means killing a living thing, then I am guilty. If it means skinning and plucking and eating the flesh, then I am also guilty.

With this confession of guilt, my critics should now be satisfied. They may not believe it, but I also had a mother and I have shown signs of compassion toward living things. As a youngster I cried when a neighbor poisoned my dog. I also cried when Bambi's mother got shot near the end of the movie.

However, I'm older now and I know better. The last time I shed tears over wildlife dying was during a movie about the draining of a marsh in southern Minnesota. As the life of the marsh flowed away, a mallard duckling—unable to fly—got squashed flat by the tracks of a bulldozer.

A sad sight, the duckling. But I was crying for the marsh as well. Maybe that's why my critics and I disagree. I've seen enough of nature, seen enough mallards to know if there's another spring there'll be another generation of mallards. Those green-headed drakes aren't chasing the hens for exercise. Come time, the hen will bring off another batch of young, thus ensuring the survival of the species.

However, the loss of a duck marsh—the mallards' home—is a different matter. Without habitat, there can't be a rebirth. When habitat is destroyed, it threatens the survival of the species.

We should be able to bag a duck without crying, but we should bawl when the marsh is drained. If you still don't understand why, please don't write.

Cooked Goose Protests

The season of harvest comes every year, an event conducted by nature as days grow shorter, air becomes cooler, and the greenery of summer turns brown and dies. In one's garden, the last fruits are plucked. Down on the farm, golden fields yield their bounty by the bushel.

The naturalist, hunter, and philosopher Aldo Leopold once observed: "There are two spiritual dangers in not owning a farm. One is the danger of supposing that breakfast comes from the grocery, and the other that heat comes from the furnace."

Americans no longer own many farms. And sure enough, Leopold's prediction has come to pass. Our breakfast sausages no longer squeal or grunt; they lie in a row in frozen silence, "Little Sizzlers" wrapped in plastic tombs. As Ed Zern once noted, we "cannot even associate a lamb chop with killing. . . . I think it is this refusal to accept death as an essential aspect of life, and man as a carnivore and therefore by deed or fiat a killer, that leads the anti-hunting sentimentalist into the idiocies of which he or she is frequently guilty."

This separation between farm and table might explain why a surplus of urban chickens, aka Canada geese, once inspired a protest in the Twin Cities. Animal rights zealots demanded the release of 260 Canada geese that were headed for slaughter and food shelves because the birds lived near the airport and posed a safety threat to airplanes that carry people.

Absurd? Of course. But Leopold warned us.

Which brings us to the Hunter's Moon rising over the land. This autumn, as hunting seasons unfold, the number of Americans who head to fields and forest will be fewer than the year before. Hunter numbers have been trending down; certainly there are fewer than a decade ago and again fewer than the decade before that. There are many reasons for the slow but steady decline in the number of hunters. But surely one of them is the slow but steady urbanization of America. As we've moved off the farm, so too we've moved away from the hunting fields.

Now, the fewer hunters that go afield, the more hunters are

viewed as an oddity on opening day, inspiring a majority of Americans to wonder, *Why do you hunt?*

It's a question that most hunters, including this one, find difficult to answer. The philosopher José Ortega y Gasset wrote that "the essence of hunting is a conscious and almost religious humbling of man which limits his superiority and lowers him toward the animal. . . . One does not hunt in order to kill; on the contrary, one kills in order to have hunted." Ortega also noted that human nature is inseparable from the hunting and killing of animals and that from this comes the most advanced aspects of human behavior.

We all are predators. And that includes you, the nonhunter. Sometimes it's a deer. Or a goose. Or a pig. A chicken. A Big Mac. Corn dog. Walleye. Escargot. If you eat veggies, you are not innocent. The fields of grain to sustain your diet have displaced countless animals.

Despite such reality, hunting critics continue to ask, "But can't you just leave your guns at home and enjoy the ducks?"

Zern answered that question: "I don't regard nature as a spectator sport. Nature, to all animals, including the human, is essentially one big food chain." Zern added that he had as much right to be a predator as the marsh hawk or skunk. "I become a part of nature, in a way I don't experience even when backpacking into the wilderness or canoeing down a whitewater river," he concluded.

Indeed, the act of hunting rekindles senses rarely used in any other human activity. A hunter notes the wind, listens for sounds, looks for movement, and smells the earth. Little of this sensory observation goes on in the football stadium on Saturday afternoons.

Ortega also wrote, "It is not essential to the hunt that it be successful. On the contrary, if the hunter's efforts were always inevitably successful it would not be the effort we call hunting, it would be something else."

New York Times columnist Nelson Bryant wrote that "most hunters are not brutish men with a lust to kill. Their relationship with wild creatures is much more complicated and sensitive than the average opponent of the pursuit would suppose." It's a message most Americans don't hear very often. Today it seems when you live away from the farm and don't understand the cycle of life, you march in protest or a file a lawsuit when a wild goose is headed for the oven.

A Hunter and Proud

In a civilized and cultivated country, wild animals only continue to exist at all when preserved by sportsmen.

—Theodore Roosevelt

Fishing often turns fast and furious in the autumn months. And every year, he makes a promise not to miss seeking browns on the Brule, the lunker walleyes in Cass, the hawg bass gorging in Minnetonka. Yet every autumn, as the nights begin to cool and the day winds of early September hint of frosty fields, rutting moons, and skies of waterfowl on the move, he does miss seeking those fish.

He is a hunter.

The autumnal metamorphosis of a hunter happens as surely as the sun sets. In the hunter's mind, for sure. Maybe it's a conditioned reflex, relating to fond memories, to youthful anticipation, including the one-on-one hunting game with the gray squirrels of Horseshoe Bend. More likely, this autumn response is merely instinctive, a primal urge to fulfill the predatory tendencies of his species, which like the wolf and lion also has the canine teeth of a meat eater.

He is a hunter.

Interestingly, the air of September is not universally sensed across the globe. Many Americans view autumn's hunting days as the season of unnecessary death for innocent beasts, of bloodlust called sport, of opening days and barbaric mentality. And, they say, hunting no longer is necessary and it should end.

This hunter has heard the charges. And examined them. He has wondered and asked, *Are they right?* He has seen death and he has caused it. He has seen lust, not for blood per se but for limits, and he's met the uncivilized who carried weapons and called themselves hunters but acted as slobs. He also has seen hunters with compassion and concern for wildlife. Love, even. He has watched hunters demand laws to protect all wildlife, including the wild game in his crosshairs. He's watched hunters pay to preserve the land where wildlife lives. He's shared their joy, their insight into things wild that only hunting delivers.

He is a hunter.

He accepts the recycling of life and the eventuality of death. For wildlife. For himself. For all that's living. If eventual death is an absolute truth—and it is—then where do his critics stand? If it's wrong to shoot a deer, is it right to kill a steer? If it's wrong to club a seal, is it right to club a calf? If it's wrong to kill living things, is it right to pull a weed? If rabbit hunting is uncivilized, is the rabbit more contented when the owl's talons rip its flesh? If consuming wild game, a renewable resource, represents a barbaric mentality, does that mean using any renewable resource is also barbaric stupidity?

Sometimes, he is a saddened hunter. If the question pertains to the survival of wildlife, the impact of his own activity is almost nil. A hunter is merely a participant in nature's own grand plan. And hunting today is regulated and monitored by the ecological sciences to sustain the hunted and the hunter as well. But little of that caretaking is understood by his critics. The critics answer with emotional charges and tearful requests from movie stars pleading for money to save seals, to save wolves, to ban trapping, to halt hunting. Send money or it will be too late.

Some people respond. They send money. They contribute because they're honestly concerned, emotionally sensitive, or suckers for half-truths and innuendos. Most of their money merely pays for the next round of advertising asking for money to save wildlife. The donors do not seem to know that there is only one way to "save" wildlife, and that is by protecting and creating wildlife habitat—a place for wildlife to live, eat, and reproduce.

They do not know that some people—hunters—have been trying to preserve wildlife habitat in these United States for more than fifty years. They do not know that some people—hunters—have contributed billions of dollars to make sure this country abounds with wild things. They do not know that these people are known collectively as America's hunters.

He is a hunter. And proud.

Please Pass the Lamb

Americans by the millions go camping every summer and roast hot dogs. No problem. We grill countless hamburgers over the campfire. Yes, great. Crispy, tender chicken over charcoal never tastes better than after a day in the great outdoors. White or dark meat? However, I recall a camping trip, which included fly-fishing for trout in South America, when a side of lamb was roasting over an open fire. No problem—ahhhh, not so fast.

To my surprise, the sight of rack of lamb over the fire made me feel uneasy. Guilty, even. And I was not alone. My fishing companions—all Minnesotans—expressed the same queasiness when I mentioned my own. Meanwhile, our Chilean fishing guides—overhearing our conversation about the "poor" lamb— seemed perplexed or, more accurately, rather amused by our reaction to a chunk of lamb over an open fire. And I knew why. A few days earlier, back at the fishing lodge, we all had feasted on roasted leg of lamb served from an iron kettle. And we all felt nothing but a full stomach.

So what gives? Our Chilean hosts must have wondered: *why are the American anglers suddenly bothered by the sight of lamb carcass cooking over hot coals?* It was a good question, and I struggled to find an answer that didn't include a huge helping of hypocrisy. After all, Herefords arrive on our plate as patties, chickens as pieces, who knows what as hot dogs.

This lamb? This lamb was different. How? This lamb walked with me to our campsite on his own four legs, led like a dog on a leash. This lamb had watched me, fly rod in hand, walk past the tents and head for a nearby trout stream. Our eyes met. The lamb suspected nothing. This lamb I had petted in an act of kindness of Judas proportions. Only I knew what was in store.

Our Chilean host, Cano St. Antoine, had earlier explained the lamb's presence. We were camping and fishing in a remote place, a coastal point called Bahia Mala in southern Chile, reachable only by traveling the Palena River to its mouth, followed by a two-hour ride in the Pacific to the mouth of an unnamed trout river. We were three hours or more from the nearest road and five hours from the nearest village. "If we want fresh meat, we must bring it that way," Cano said. He pointed to the lamb's neck and, using his finger like a knife, demonstrated how the lamb's death would be as quick and painless as he could make it. "We raise millions of them," he said, pointing toward the pending main course. In other words, one dead lamb, no big deal.

I had to ask myself: *what's so bothersome about the demise of one lamb when every day millions of animals in the United States and around the world face the same end?* As a longtime hunter I have accepted and played the role of predator. I have killed fleeing pheasants and brown-eyed deer. Was taking a knife to a walleye any different than taking a knife to a lamb?

Maybe it was my power over the lamb that was troublesome. Lord knows, plenty of deer, pheasants, and fish have escaped my capture. The lamb, however, didn't have a chance. Yet I was also quite sure my fellow predators in the animal kingdom never struggled with the idea of killing to eat. A wolf or coyote would inhale that lamb and its mother too. Good eatin.' Next?

Perhaps we humans as predators have become, well, rusty. Soft, maybe. Or shielded from reality. When I was a farm kid, my job was to behead live chickens to fill the family's freezer for the winter. Today there's no chicken head to remove; we have legs and wings, breasts and thighs nicely wrapped in cellophane. We don't kill anymore. We merely consume. We don't kill cows; we eat Big Macs. There's no petting zoo at Burger King. Some folks contend animals have rights the same as humans. Anti-hunting protesters believe they march with clean hands; they might eat meat or vegetables or walk in leather shoes, but they kill nothing.

I must confess I'll never forget that lamb. It made me think about my own role as a predator with canine teeth.

"Grab a plate," somebody said. We gathered around the campfire. I looked again at the lamb. Now it was just a piece of meat.

I had to admit, it tasted pretty good.

Mr. President, Eat the Damned Turkey

On national holidays, you'd think our presidents would be honest and up front with their messages to the nation. You'd think. How about it, Mr. President: to celebrate Thanksgiving, why don't you and the missus eat that danged turkey? But no. Instead, Mr. President, you declare some kind of turkey pardon so the fat thing goes off to die of obesity.

I suppose this ridiculous ceremony to pardon a farmyard turkey shouldn't be getting me so upset. But really, millions of us Americans are expected to chew on dead turkey for Thanksgiving. So what does our president do? He sends his turkey to a petting zoo and makes the rest of us feel like serial bird killers. What's with that, Mr. President? Some kind of federalized guilt trip?

Roughly 46 million turkeys—dead ones—are on America's Thanksgiving tables every year; 22 million die to celebrate Christmas, and 19 million turkeys give it up for Easter. According to industry surveys, 95 percent of the nation's Thanksgiving dinners consist of dead turkey. With all due respect, Mr. President, if I'm killing a turkey, my president should too. It's the American way.

Worse, this silly pardon tradition is spreading to state governments as well. Minnesota Governor Tim Walz chose to pardon his bird too. The press was all over that. I think I read that the governor's turkey would later appear on a different Thanksgiving table. In the spirit of "all one Minnesota," he should have looked at the turkey and said "this sucker is heading for the oven on Summit Avenue." The press would have been all over that too.

President Harry Truman was the first to send his Thanksgiving dinner away from the White House alive. Every president since has done the same. Hauling a farm turkey to the nation's capital was a promotion started in 1947 by the National Turkey Federation, an organization of turkey growers. The idea was to give the president a complimentary turkey so as to remind all Americans they should buy one. Tell me how this annual Rose Garden ceremony makes sense. The turkey growers want us to gorge ourselves on their turkey carcasses; meanwhile, the president plays the politically correct game and sends his turkey away "to live out the rest of its years."

Oh, give me a break. White domestic turkeys are delicious, but the big ol' bird is too fat to fly and too dumb to run, and if it rains, it'll look up and drown. You can't pet a tom turkey; it'll peck a hole in the president's blue suit coat.

Can't we play it straight, Mr. President? Farm-raised turkeys are for eating, not petting. Instead of pardons, why not use the Rose Garden ceremony to remind all Americans that their meat isn't always wrapped in cellophane? Writer James Swan had a better honest idea. He said, "If we're going to honor a turkey at Thanksgiving, then let's honor the original bird, the wild turkey."

The wild turkey was most likely present for the first Thanksgiving in 1621. The wild turkey was almost hunted to extinction until America discovered its conservation conscience. Today, wild turkey populations are thriving in forty-nine of the fifty states. So, Mr. President, why not celebrate Thanksgiving by reminding Americans we have restored one of the country's originals, the wild turkey? Sadly, most Americans haven't heard the story. You could spread a great conservation message, Mr. President.

Just do it. Eat that damned turkey.

Turkey Track Club

This story begins—as good stories often do—with a spring turkey hunt in South Dakota's Black Hills. On an April morning in 1974, there were three of us in the predawn darkness quietly walking atop a ridge of ponderosa pines. Our destination was to get close to the source of a gobble heard the night before. Little did we realize or even imagine back then that our turkey hunt would become a historic moment in the annals of wild turkey conservation.

The short version goes like this: when the morning hunt was over forty-five years ago, it was the unplanned beginning of a hunting camp called the Turkey Track Club, located in the Black Hills near Piedmont, South Dakota. Those hunters who came to Turkey Track Club were primarily Minnesotans. After experiencing the pursuit of wild turkeys, they returned home inspired to improve turkey populations and someday have a hunting season there. (At the time, Minnesota had a struggling turkey population and no hunting season.) In addition, it was their turkey hunting experience at Turkey Track Club that led to the creation of the first National Wild Turkey Federation chapters in two states, Minnesota and South Dakota.

Rather amazing, yes. If anything, this story once again proves the magnetism of the wild turkey and how the bird can turn strangers into lifelong friends. That's how I met a South Dakota fella named John Hauer. And this encounter is where this story really starts.

John Hauer and I were both turkey nuts, but we didn't know each other. I was writing outdoor columns for the *Minneapolis Tribune*, and John, president of a business college in Rapid City, read my Black Hills turkey yarns. One day he sent a letter inviting me to a spring hunt on his ranch. I accepted, and we immediately clicked as friends. We actually thought we were pretty awesome at calling gobblers and began to offer our turkey guiding services for free. A couple of John's friends turned us down when we said we'd start at 3 AM. In the meantime, I was sharing my Black Hills turkey hunting exploits in the newspaper back in Minnesota. Finally one friend, Bobby Nybo, of Red Wing, agreed to fly to Rapid City and try this thing called turkey hunting.

On that April morning, in the predawn darkness, we picked up Bobby at the Covered Wagon motel in Piedmont. It was Bobby's first visit to the Black Hills and his first turkey hunt. However, having landed the night before at the Rapid City airport, Bobby had yet to actually see the hills in daylight as we walked a ridge in darkness. Still before dawn, we propped Bobby against a ponderosa pine and pointed in the general direction of the gobbler's roost. Soon, the first gobble of the day echoed off the ridge. Then, more gobbles.

John and I answered with sweet yelps as the eastern sky brightened and bird life sounded in the hills. I have long forgotten all the details, but I do know the gobbler flew to the ground and walked into shotgun range. Bobby took aim and the hunt was over. But not really. As Bobby kneeled alongside a mature Merriam's gobbler, admiring its beauty, he for the first time could see for miles from the high ridge, admiring also the beauty of the Black Hills.

For the Turkey Track Club, the rest is history. The next spring, Bobby returned and fifteen more Minnesotans came to camp for a taste of turkey hunting, something none of them had ever done. To accommodate the hunters, the Covered Wagon motel agreed to provide meals and rooms and set up a makeshift lodge atmosphere. To manage everyone in the field, John and I recruited a few local turkey hunters to act as guides. We created a three-day package spread over four days, comprised of three mornings and three afternoons of hunting.

From the very beginning, we practiced fair chase and emphasized following the state's hunting laws. South Dakota turkey regulations allowed for the use of high-powered rifles to kill a turkey. We did not. Shotguns or archery only was the rule at Turkey Track Club. Why? We wanted our club members to experience the thrill of a gobbler coming to the call. That doesn't happen if you whack the bird at a hundred yards with a .30-06 deer rifle.

John and I chose the name Turkey Track Club because we believed turkey hunters were a unique fraternity, a "club" so to speak. When you share the experience of rising long before dawn to hear the wind whispering in the hills, when you hunker along in a dark woods, trudging up and down rugged terrain, when you stalk the grandest of all game—the gobbler—well, welcome to the "Club."

Turkey Track Club membership, written by Ron in 1975 and given to any hunter who attended the South Dakota club.

Well-known sports retailer Bud Burger with Black Hills gobbler and guide Ron Schara.

I also had learned long ago that a relationship with the wild turkey is extremely contagious. As a young writer, fresh out of journalism school at Iowa State University, my first job in 1966 was with the South Dakota Department of Game, Fish, and Parks. In the spring of 1967 I was introduced to turkey hunting by the department's deer and turkey biologist, Art Richardson. On that morning, I heard my first turkey gobble, saw my first wild turkey, and killed my first gobbler, a jake. By 1968 I was writing for the Minneapolis paper, but I never missed a Black Hills spring turkey season for fifty years.

My location may explain why Turkey Track Club gave birth to the first National Wild Turkey Federation chapter in Minnesota. In 1977 club members returned to Minnesota enthusiastic about restoring turkeys in their home state. I was already a NWTF member, and I called a meeting of a few club members. We gathered at Bobby Nybo's restaurant in Red Wing on a winter evening. By the time the meeting ended, we had created the state's first NWTF chapter and I was elected its first president. We began with a fundraising banquet in the Twin Cities. Minnesota had never held a turkey season, and most Minnesotans were unaware of the joys of turkey hunting. It didn't matter. The first banquet was a huge success, raising more than $10,000, which was an NWTF record at the time. Our guest speaker was Ben Rogers Lee, a giant of a man and an Alabama turkey hunting celebrity. The next year, 1978, the young, personable turkey calling expert Rob Keck was our guest speaker; he would go on to be executive director of NWTF.

Our chapter goal was simple: restore turkeys and turkey hunting in Minnesota. I remember a conversation with the Minnesota Department of Natural Resources' chief of wildlife, Roger Holmes, during which I urged him to do more to increase wild turkey populations. He said his wildlife budget was already spread too thin. "If you want more turkeys, you raise the money," he replied.

So we did. With the dollars our banquets brought in, the first NWTF chapter became a major donor to pay for the DNR's trap and transplant crew to move wild birds into new habitat. In its first six years, the one and only NWTF chapter in Minnesota donated $30,000 to the DNR's trap and transplant operations. Some chapter money also was used to purchase food plots, back when we thought turkeys needed support to survive the winter season.

When the DNR's turkey restoration efforts ended years later, local NWTF chapters had contributed upward of $500,000 to move birds and fill the state's abundant turkey habitat.

Today there are seventy-five Minnesota NWTF chapters with nearly ten thousand members (ninth in the nation). Together the chapters have donated thousands of dollars to conserve or enhance more than 51,000 acres of turkey habitat to secure the future of wild turkeys and hunting. It's a modern-day conservation success story. Minnesota's wild turkey population is into the tens of thousands of birds, including areas in the far north as well as the suburbs of Minneapolis–St. Paul.

Tom Glines, a longtime Minnesota NWTF officer and now one of the organization's directors of development, said, "the first few local chapters and their contribution to the state's trap and transplant program are the reason we enjoy the abundance of birds we have today."

The very first turkey season in Minnesota was held in 1978, and four hundred lucky hunters received a license in a DNR drawing. I wasn't one of them. Those four hundred hunters bagged ninety-four birds. Minnesota turkey hunters now number more than 46,000, taking roughly 6,000 gobblers a season.

The future for the wild turkey in Minnesota is very secure, but it all started on that April morning in the Black Hills. After Turkey Track Club members organized the first Minnesota NWTF chapter, the next year we gathered in Rapid City and started the first South Dakota NWTF chapter.

Turkey Track Club continues. Dating back to 1974, the club is one of the oldest hunting camps in America and still introducing hunters—young and old—to the beauty of South Dakota's Black Hills. Yup, that gobbler is an inspiration that just keeps on giving.

Sorta True Fish Tales

How to Know a Fishing Expert

There weren't any fishing experts in my hometown that I remember, except maybe Bobby Brouillet. Bobby Brouillet could hand tie trout flies, and he bragged about it around school. Bobby was a few years older than Joe Ball and me. He could wrap feathers on a hook and, at the same time, spew a blue streak about the new pattern he was concocting and why it ought to fool the trout at Livingood Springs. We always paid close attention to Bobby's fishing advice. Like I said, he was the only fishing expert we knew.

One evening on the banks of Livingood Springs, Joe Ball and I had Bobby Brouillet convinced that the raspy buzz he was hearing on the far bank was a rattlesnake. Timber rattler, we called them. Joe Ball and I laughed, but we didn't brag much about our practical joke. Brouillet's reputation could have been ruined if we'd told of how the expert didn't know the difference between the buzzing tail of a rattler and the buzz of flying grasshoppers. Besides, Brouillet still tied danged-good trout flies and gave them to us for free.

Joe Ball and I always thought we were pretty good at trout catching, and we told each other that. However, we didn't brag much about our trout expertise unless we got a limit or landed a trout that deserved to be seen in the local newspaper.

That's the difference between an expert angler and a good one. An expert tells others how it's done; good fisherfolk never tell anything. Fact is, I've always been suspicions of anglers who are eager to be known as fishing experts. Of late, that seems to be the aspiration of every angler, to become an expert by listening to others who've claimed the title in seminars. When fishing fever arrives in

Minnesota, long before the walleye opener, the wannabe experts are a dime a dozen, each anxious to stand before the piscatorial losers and talk of their angling savvy.

Don't misunderstand. There's nothing dumb about milking the knowledge of experts. And some of what is said is worth hearing. What's more, good golly, one evening I was invited to speak at Mount Olivet Lutheran Church to a gathering of angling hopefuls. To my utter surprise, I was introduced as a fishing expert. Standing in a house of the Lord as the announced fishing expert is pretty heavy stuff. I mean, it's possible the first-ever fishing seminar in history was given by St. Peter, the Fisherman Disciple.

Quickly, I assured the audience that I was a long ways from a piscatorial guru. There's a song that goes: Oh Lord, it's hard to be humble. Correction: It's not hard to be humble if you pursue fish. I learned this lesson the easy way one day on the banks of a trout pool on Livingood Springs.

Since I saw myself as an above-average trout seeker, I dressed the part, adorned in camouflaged garb so the trout couldn't see me. I also carried the trappings of the trout elite: bamboo fly rod, bamboo fish creel, hip boots, and a high nose. I figured any trout fisher who showed up on the stream with less was a lightweight who'd be lucky to catch a cold.

One morning I met one of these lightweights at the big trout pool. He was dressed in striped overalls and five-buckle rubber boots. Both were stained as a consequence of standing near the rear end of milk cows on a cement barn floor. He was sitting on a log watching his red-white bobber, the size of a softball, floating in the trout pool. His fishing rod was one of those old solid steel jobs, complete with a $1.98 reel filled with yards of fifty-pound test black line of slightly less diameter than baling twine. A couple of old five-gallon cream cans were standing behind him.

As I approached, I had to stop myself from laughing. Here was a picture of trout fishing ineptitude. How not to fool a trout, huh? Just to be polite, I asked him how he was doing.

"Got a few," he replied, pointing to one of the cream cans. Surprised by his answer, I had to take a look. The tall can was quarter filled with chubs and suckers. Wasn't a trout among them. *No sur-*

prise there, I thought to myself, *ain't no eagle-eyed trout ever gonna inhale a hook tied to black fifty-pound line.*

Without a word I moseyed over to peek into the other cream can. Curled in the bottom was one of the nicest brown trout I'd ever seen. "Did you catch this trout?" I asked in disbelief.

"Yup," said the farmer. "Took a gob of worms I dug out of the manure pile." He held up a Folgers coffee can. "They're the best, these manure worms."

Before I could walk away he showed me how he gobbed the worms on a hook. He showed me how deep he was fishing. It takes a lot of patience to catch trout that big, he instructed. As I walked away, I said, "That's a dandy trout, my friend." I don't think he noticed my fishing outfit. Fishing experts don't have to dress the part.

Uncle Bob's Biggest Trout

Angling memories, they flow like rivers. Timeless and endearing, they wind through an angler's lifetime, carrying the joys—or the burdens—of catching fish. Bend after bend . . . of times when the fishing was good, but the catching was not. Of glorious moments with fish as large as an angler's greatest exaggerations. They also tell of relationships. Those seasons of sharing a boat, a riverbank, a trout pool. Casting toward a common goal for common dreams. Of being part of the fraternity that finds the pursuit of fish worth the price of biting flies, torn waders, and backlashes.

My days of fishing with Uncle Bob remind me of the bonding. For example, I was taught that a trout's diet is about ninety percent insects. Uncle Bob impressed me with this lesson early on. When we fished together, Uncle Bob would walk ahead of me, his bamboo fly rod whipping back and forth as he expertly cast for elusive brown trout, the wisest fish in the stream. He always let me, then a twelve-year-old fly-fishing novice, tag along and watch. Uncle Bob was my idol. He was the best there was, a master angler with a matched fly, stalking the northeast Iowa streams such as Bloody Run or Waterloo Creek. To make sure I didn't forget, Uncle Bob often told me how good he was.

Sometimes on the stream, Uncle Bob would suggest that I should use a dark fly or a light-colored one. Then he'd point me downstream while he moseyed upstream to where the smartest browns lurked. While I floundered with my fly rod, Uncle Bob would suddenly holler, ordering me to come running as fast as I could in hip boots. As usual, he was tangling with another big brown and needed help netting the fish. After the beautiful brown was safely in the net, Uncle Bob would graciously show me his secret fly. "Here's what you shoulda been using," he scolded. Gosh, I wished I could choose flies like he did.

As creeks turn into rivers, fish tales also change. "They last longer and resist the truth," former vice president Walter Mondale once mused.

Just like the day the *Marquette Times* ran a picture of Uncle Bob holding a huge brown trout. Oh, it was a big fish, a seven-pounder or so. And Uncle Bob looked pretty proud holding up that fish for the news photographer. The headline read, "A Local Boy Catches Huge Trout from Bloody Run." Uncle Bob didn't mind the publicity. Making the news like that merely solidified his reputation as one of the best fly fishermen in Clayton County, which is what he said he was all along. It was a harmless exercise, showing off that giant trout, although Uncle Bob never did actually catch it. Oh sure, Uncle Bob knew that big ol' German brown lived in Bloody Run. At least he said he did. And he probably would have caught that trophy eventually.

But the real fish story was: a mink had caught it first.

As it happened, Uncle Bob had come by shortly after the mink landed the trout. The mink took off without its catch. That big ol' brown was still fresh, with only an eye or two missing. Uncle Bob said a mink always eats the eyes first. Anyway, Uncle Bob picked up the beautiful trout and decided that such a trophy ought to be seen by his fishing buddies, who didn't believe there were such giants swimming in Bloody Run.

As Uncle Bob started hiking back to town, carrying the trout, he was following the railroad tracks and generally minding his own business when a crew of railroad workers passed by. They were watching Uncle Bob and that huge fish. As he walked along, Uncle Bob explained later, he wiggled the trout as if it were freshly caught and still alive. Just an innocent little gesture, for sure. However, before Uncle Bob could explain, the railroad crew was admiring the fish and shouting praises about Uncle Bob's angling ability. What could he say? He didn't want to disappoint anybody. So he said he caught it, which is what they wanted to hear anyway.

A local reporter got wind of the big fish (or somebody leaked the story), and pretty soon Uncle Bob was giving interviews and having his picture taken for the next week's edition. To this day, nobody for miles around Marquette has been the wiser. *What the local folk don't know won't hurt 'em.* Uncle Bob still enjoys a reputation as a fishing expert. He did say, if that trout had been a state record, he never would have claimed it.

It's important for fisherfolk to have scruples.

How to Name Fish

I once caught a fish that had a tail something like a golden retriever but upside down. There were no legs, however, just fins. The fish is called a dogfish. A dogfish? Did some canine lover name this fish to get even with feline fans who have the catfish? A catfish has whiskers at least, but what's doglike about a dogfish?

According to fish scientists who are expected to know these things, the dogfish got its name because the fish makes a croaking sound when out of the water. The noise apparently was like a barking dog. It seems a dogfish also has an air bladder that functions like a lung and therefore can make a gasping or belching sound. What breed of dog bark wasn't noted.

What about the names given to other fish? Here's a short course on fish naming:

Redhorse (sucker): A red color appears on the fins. Fine, but how does that explain the horse part? When the redhorse spawns, it tends to roll or leap along the water surface. Somebody sometime apparently thought the fish's action imitated a running or bucking horse. Brilliant.

Dolly Varden trout: A colorful western trout species, the Dolly Varden was named after a character in a western book. Dolly was a colorful dance hall girl. Don't know if she had a face—or a body—like a trout.

Brown trout: There was a debate over naming this popular fish when it first arrived in the United States. The first brown trout were a gift of a German government official named Von Behr, and it was suggested that they ought to be called the Von Behr trout. However, before the name became official, Scotland also sent some brown trout, called Loch Leven because the trout came from a lake with the same name. A great debate followed. One side argued for the Loch Leven name; another opted for German brown trout. Today most anglers simply call it a brown trout. Von Behr lost out completely.

Sheepshead: If you have a rich imagination this fish kinda looks like a sheep's head. Same with the buffalo fish. Its humplike back is not unlike that of a bison. Again, use your imagination.

Walleye: Minnesota's official state fish gets its name because of its enlarged eyes for seeing under low light. Those eyes appear to be glazed or "walleyed."

Largemouth and smallmouth bass: No mystery here—the largemouth bass has a larger mouth than the smallmouth bass. Not even close.

Miscellaneous species: Stonerollers roll stones, and sticklebacks have sharp spines . . . you know where.

Muskie: The name is derived from the Ojibwe maashkinoozhe, which means great size and strength, a "great pike." Maashkinoozhe is also spelled *muskellunge*, but today's fisherfolk just say "muskie."

Dog salmon: In Alaska the dog salmon is so called because the Inuit usually fed the fish to their dogs. Makes sense.

Parrot fish: A Florida fish that was so named because it appears to have the face of a parrot. More imagination needed here.

Great northern pike: When early Euro-American anglers, familiar with a small pike that roamed lakes on the East Coast, tangled with a big brother pike in Minnesota, they named it the great northern pike.

Personally, I like the unofficial version of how the great northern got its name. A long time ago, it seems a fellow was found sitting on the railroad tracks with a fishing pole in his hands. Asked why he was sitting there, he replied: "I'm waiting to catch a Great Northern."

The Fish of Ten Thousand Casts

Fishing for muskies is like writing love letters that are never mailed.
Your chances of success are limited but there's pleasure in the ritual.

—Nelson Bryant, *New York Times*

The first fishing book I wrote was a doozy. It was about the muskie, a fish I knew nothing about. However, I also observed what the muskie did to usually normal anglers. I watched the hands of veteran muskie seekers quiver and shake while holding the fish, even a small one. I realized then and there that if a fish could make a grown man's body shake, the same fish could inspire me to write a book about the most mysterious fish in fresh water. The title was *Muskie Mania.*

In all of fresh water, there's no fish like a muskie. It's big. And toothy. It's the ruler of its watery domain and fears nothing smaller than itself. It's a fish with an attitude. But there's more to this fish story. Anglers might relish walleye or praise pike. Bass might be fun to catch and bluegills delicious to eat. But only the muskie can with impunity cause anglers' knees to quiver. Of all Minnesota's game fish, only the muskie comes with its own mystique, a celebrity super fish sustained over the ages by those who seek to catch it. Of these powers, fish legends are made.

As early as 1891 a Minnesota newspaper, the *Hubbard County Clipper*, classified the muskie as "the king of freshwater fish." In 1889 a Colonel Harding, who was best known for capturing Jefferson Davis during the Civil War, traveled to Minnesota to fish for muskies in the Mantrap chain near Park Rapids. He reported catching three hundred muskies. If true, that's a remarkable achievement.

In July 1955 a story broke from Leech Lake that still belongs in *Ripley's Believe It or Not*. It was called the Muskie Rampage. And there was no explanation. In two days, twenty-seven muskies were caught on Leech, the largest forty-two pounds, six ounces. Within a week, a total of 140 muskie catches were reported. When the so-called rampage ended, 163 muskies, the largest forty-three pounds, were killed, hung on hooks, and photographed for proof. The picture still appears now and then, fodder for more mystique.

It's generally understood that it's not easy to catch a muskie. A popular adage is: it takes ten thousand casts to catch a muskie. Plus you can add about a hundred hours of patience. The Minnesota Department of Natural Resources did a survey of muskie seekers and found it takes more than a hundred hours of effort on average to catch a legal muskie. Compare that catch rate to the bluegill, at one fish for every seventy-five minutes.

As you might imagine, the angler who catches the largest muskie in American history would become famous, maybe even rich. It might even be tempting to lie to hold such great piscatorial honor. Enter a New York fisherman, Art Lawton, who for thirty years held the world-record muskie title. Countless stories were written about the sixty-nine-pound, fifteen-ounce muskie that Lawton landed on September 22, 1957, in the St. Lawrence River.

When I was writing *Muskie Mania*, I called Lawton, and he was kind enough to retell the story of that famous catch. Bingo, he was in yet another fishing book, mine. Turned out to be just a fish story. Somebody found the holes in his tall tale. Sadly, Lawton died a lonely outcast in Chicago, although he might hold the record for the biggest fish tale of all time.

Truth is, muskies are capable of reaching large sizes. The fish can live for more than thirty years. Some anglers confuse northern pike with muskies. Best description is a muskie has dark spots on a light background while a pike shows light spots on a dark background. It's also true if you hook a muskie—well, you'll know it.

It's impossible to write about muskies in Minnesota without mentioning the name Gil Hamm. He loved muskies. The St. Paul contractor was dissatisfied with the poor muskie fishing in Minnesota. He complained, but state fisheries folks largely ignored him. Not to be denied, Gil Hamm organized a group of fellow anglers into Muskies, Inc., in 1966. Today there are Muskies, Inc., chapters in more than fifteen states, with thousands of members who preach catch and release of such a trophy fish and pay for muskie stocking and research.

Gil was a doer who believed the best way to improve your own fishing is to do it yourself. It remains good advice to this day. If you wanna catch a muskie, make your own casts.

Why I Fish

Why do I fish?

It's a fair question but it's not an easy answer. For one thing, we anglers are seldom asked to explain what keeps us casting, keeps us hoping to catch something. It's no mystery to us. Perhaps the only people who are puzzled by fishing are those who don't do it.

It's been said the essence of fishing is much more than casting or retrieving or playing your catch. It's the wind in your face, they say; the sound of awakening birds as the sun peeks over the horizon. In every fishy place there is magic and mystery. The quest to unlock the secrets takes you to some of the world's garden spots. And let's not forget the pure joy of catching, that moment when a fishing dream is on the end of the line. Memories are made of this.

Fishing is also a teacher. The lessons learned in a fishing boat are not lost on land, either. Patience is required—but patience pays. To fish is also to be humbled—not once but time and again. Frankly, lessons in humility help keep life itself in perspective.

Sure, some of us tend to exaggerate a fish or two, it's said. But for every tale of giant whoppers, there's the true stories about the one that got away.

There's also an eternal side to this pursuit we call angling. It's a pursuit of a lifetime. You're never too young to start, and you're never too old to quit. I like that. As my own opening days wind down to a precious few, it's nice to know I'll be there as long as I can. As long as I can bait a hook and make a cast. As long as I am living, I'll be fishing.

Greatest Fish Story Ever Told

Late in the summer of 1959 Ron Weber ambled into the Dove Clothing establishment in downtown Duluth, Minnesota. A Finlander, Aleks Kyyhkynen, owned the store, which specialized in plaid shirts and other working wear for north woods lumberjacks. Ron Weber, though a local, was not a logger, however. He was an avid fisherman and sales rep for fishing tackle companies. "I'm looking for that Finlander plug," Weber inquired. The store owner nodded, reaching under the counter for two minnow-shaped lures of different sizes. They had been sent to the clothier from the old country by his Finnish relatives. They weren't cheap, not at $1.95 and $2.25. "You want them or no?" Kyyhkynen said with a grunt.

Weber didn't hesitate. He already had watched a fishing companion catch walleyes with the Finlander plug that had been sent by a relative who worked at the American consulate in Helsinki. To get such a Finnish lure himself, Weber was told to go to Dove Clothing. The rumor was Kyyhkynen had a few of the gizmos behind the counter. Weber picked up the lures. Both were handmade of light balsa wood. They had a name: Rapala (pronounced RAPpala, not raPALA).

So begins one of the most amazing fishing stories in American history. Millions of Rapalas are sold in the United States every year; upward of 20 million are sold worldwide. For decades, every Rapala sold in the United States passed through Ron Weber's hands via his Twin Cities company, Normark Corporation.

However, this is not a tale about a mass-produced chunk of wood with hooks. Rapala has a storybook history. The first lures were hand carved by a Finnish fisherman, Lauri Rapala, who had more talent than capital. They were made of balsa, wrapped in foil from pieces of candy, and sealed by melting old film negatives. The scale marks were made with a nailhead. Rapala created the first one in 1936 after watching minnows swim as he rowed a fishing boat. There were just two colors, gold and silver, because those were the only colors of foil in the candy store. That's also why the original models had stars on the sides. Lauri Rapala didn't want stars; the candy store did.

In the fall of 1959, Weber sent a handwritten letter to Rapala ordering a thousand lures and asking for exclusive distribution rights in the United States and Canada. A month later, Rapala sent a letter agreeing to a one-year term. Almost overnight, Weber and his business partner, Ray Ostrom, had sold all one thousand lures. "I ordered another five thousand by letter. Lauri wrote back telling me that five thousand was his entire production for a year," Weber said.

Then Marilyn Monroe got into the act. The actress was featured on the cover of the August 17, 1962, edition of *Life* magazine. Millions of Americans picked up the issue to see more of Marilyn. However, the magazine also featured another story. It was entitled "A Lure Fish Can't Pass Up."

Unbeknownst to Weber and Ostrom, the editor of *Life* magazine was an avid fisherman. He had heard about a little ol' man in Finland who made hand carved fishing lures and sent a writer to find out more. By mere coincidence, the story of Lauri Rapala and his fish-catching lure appeared in the same edition with Marilyn Monroe's memoirs. Almost immediately, anglers across America wanted a Rapala and found out who had them. "We were getting bags of

Ron Weber, discoverer of the Rapala lure, with Ron.

mail every day," Weber said. "People would send cash or a check with instructions to send as many Rapalas as the money would buy. We had orders for three million lures by direct mail."

There was only one problem. Weber and Ostrom didn't have many Rapalas. "We couldn't fill ten percent of the orders," said Weber. Still, the demand for the lure didn't subside. Tackle stores were renting the lures for five dollars a day with a twenty-dollar deposit. Other lure companies tried making look-alikes. Weber and Ostrom had another idea. They offered to help Lauri Rapala build new company facilities and expand annual production from 150,000 to 350,000 lures. The rest, as they say, is history.

Sadly, Lauri Rapala never realized how popular his lure was with American anglers. He died in 1974. He was sixty-nine, but he wasn't a poor fisherman anymore.

Over the years, the original Rapala has changed little. Although machines help carve the balsa bodies, each lure still is hand tested in a water tank in the Finnish factory. And it still catches fish.

My Fishy Poem

Those of us who fish, it seems
Are always chasing lunker dreams.
But those we catch
we tend to keep.
So there are fewer lunkers for others to seek.

If you want fish to eat, the smallest are best;
They fit in the pan and pass every test.
Big fish are for pictures and stories at night
To show off for friends
and declare bragging rights.
Why mount real fish for the wall
when replicas will do?
Just use a photo and molded graphite;
Add some paint and some glue.

Do we really need a law to do what's right?
To recycle the big ones for another day's fight?
Big fish are rare, rarer than gold
To be honored and revered
like anything old.

If we release all the lunkers,
there'll be more big ones to find
And our luck will get better;
I hope you don't mind.
We can't have it both ways;
this fact should be clear.
You wanna chance for a big fish?
Or keep waiting for years?

Ron the fly angler, Star Tribune
promo shot, ca. 1970–73.

The Love of Openers

*They say the pursuit of fish is an eternal search. They say it's never
too late to begin, young or old. They say the last fishing day of one's
life will pass with questions unanswered. I choose to believe that.
And it all starts with opening day.*

When you say "the opener" in Minnesota, nobody mistakenly
thinks of the Twins baseball season opener. No, the opener is the
first day of a long-running love story: Minnesotans and walleyes.

Opening day means busy bait shops, busy resorts, family re-
unions, heavy northbound traffic, crowded boat ramps, and so
forth. When an estimated five hundred thousand Minnesotans go
fishing at once, the scenarios can be endless. Minnesota might not
be at the top of many lists, but we're number one in fishing license
sales per capita.

Opening day is not just about fishing; it's more important than
that. Someone (me, I think) once wrote there are three major holidays in Minnesota: Christmas, New Year's, and Opening Day. Indeed, very few of our United States celebrate a fishing date on the
calendar, let alone turn it into a statewide party from the governor
on down. Wisconsin has a walleye opener, but who knew? Motels
aren't full; resorts aren't packed. In northern Minnesota on opening weekend, you'd better have reservations. However, Minnesota
and Wisconsin often share one common fishing result on opening
day: our governors get skunked.

The most significant downside to opening day is that it often
falls on Mother's Day. This confluence was nobody's idea. Blame
the calendar, tradition, and walleye spawning cycles. This clash of
special occasions never would have bothered my mother, however.
She always went fishing on Mother's Day.

Is this grandiose view of opening day some romanticized fish
tale, the dreams of a night crawler hunter? I have no proof, but I
think not. Rather, I'd like to believe the opener is a bonding moment in Minnesota. Rarely are so many of us wondering the same
thing: where are the walleyes? On opening weekend, we all find

ourselves in the same boat, floating together in an eternal quest to fool the pea-sized brain of a fish. Neither wind nor waves nor snow showers detract us. We have learned to pack snowmobile suits.

Opening day fishing rules tend to be flexible. If the walleyes are biting, the most successful anglers are allowed and expected to gloat or brag or both. To catch nothing is not fun, but to get skunked on opening day is worse. God-awful. Depressing. We've all been there.

Oh, the memories. Hey, maybe that's it? Opening day is a maker of memories, memories to be told and retold as the fishing seasons go by.

I'll never forget that fisherman on Lake Mary who caught a dandy eight-pound walleye on the morning of the opener. He was so proud. Again and again, he'd lift up the fish on a stringer for all to see. Then it happened. As he hoisted up the lunker to show it off, the big fish made a sudden flop and the stringer slipped out of the angler's hand. In the next instant, the trophy walleye slowly began swimming toward the depths, stringer and all. The panicked angler quickly slipped off his coat, followed by his shirt, pants, and shoes. He dived overboard. Watching in horror, I told my dad and brother that we'd better head over to the fella's boat, otherwise we might be witnessing a drowning. Opening day water is too cold to swim in for long. As we quickly motored over, the chilled fisherman returned to the surface with nothing but goose bumps. We helped him get back into his boat. "Just as I reached for the stringer, the fish flicked its tail and was gone," he cried.

My memory of the 2014 Minnesota opener also has not faded, and will not fade ever. I can still see my younger brother, Robert, on the end of the dock waiting for a bite on Bowstring Lake. He was wrapped in a blanket and sitting in a wheelchair. A year earlier bro' Robert was running his own boat and declaring himself to be the "Walleye Whisperer." This was before the cancer in his brain took over. My, my, isn't it remarkable how fishing openers and lives change from one season to the next? Robert died about a month later, July 2, 2014. We miss him, of course. But most of all, he's missed on opening day.

My grandson, Jake, also has missed several opening day get-togethers. Seems there's always a baseball practice or baseball game

Grandson Jake on his first fishing trip with grandpa in front of TV cameras.

scheduled by a coach or somebody in sports. Who would do this? Who would require a kid to come to practice and, therefore, not be with the family for the biggest sporting event of the year, opening day? Good grief, what were they thinking? Clearly we need a new law: opening weekend is for mothers and fishing only.

As I ponder the many openers I've enjoyed, I also wonder about how many openers I have left. There's no answer, of course, and that's probably just as well. It's not something I like to think about, but, well, you know. I'm certain, however, that my many openers now outnumber those I have left. Oh well. So be it. That's the way it goes. That's life. Anglers must always be optimistic. Pass the minnows. I'm expecting a bite.

The (Sorta) True Story about Gary Roach

Sometimes the best fishing stories are actually true. Sometimes you really do catch what you deserve. Sometimes you don't have to be lucky at catching walleyes because you really are good at what you do. And sometimes nice guys really do finish first.

Move over, Mother Goose. Step aside, Mickey Mouse and Popeye. Those aren't the only fairy tales that come true. The story of Gary Roach is also a dream life.

Born in a Minnesota spruce swamp. Learned to fish good the hard way and with practice. Probably by skipping school. Ran a gas station. Wasn't good at it. Ended up in the fishing business. Busy guide. Nice catches. Small pay. Big tips, sometimes.

Fast-forward years later: big sponsors, good money, tournament victories, thousands of fans, and a nickname only he can live up to—Mr. Walleye.

The last time I looked, Gary Roach was still in the back of the boat, loving every minute, catching fish, wondering why his partner couldn't keep up. His thirst to catch one more fish knows no quenching. What else would you expect from Mr. Walleye?

Oh yes, the years have slid by now. Gary's beard is white and his eyes are wrinkled by decades of wind and sun on the water. He's always been a kind soul and still is. These details do not explain why many of his close friends call him "Rotten Roach." Granted, the name has a nice lilt: R-R. Rotten Roach. Let me just say Rotten Roach has deserved the handle. In a fishing boat, Gary Roach would do anything to catch more fish than his mother. He'd be rotten but nice about it, of course.

In the world of competitive walleye tournaments, Gary reached the top of the mountain as Walleye Angler of the Year in 1991. The title goes to the angler with the highest total weight of walleyes in four tournaments. Roach's winning total—more than 173 pounds—includes a record fifteen-fish, eighty-seven-pound catch in Lake Erie.

One year I joined him as a tournament partner and fishing writer. My goal was to write about the life and times of tournaments, the behind-the-scenes stuff. Instead, we fished smart and hard and ended up winning our division, then losing the championship by less than a pound or two. I was voted rookie of the year, of all things.

Gary Roach is still fishing. He seeks no other vices. There aren't many anglers who can scratch out a living between the gunwales. For one thing, the fish have minds of their own. And the elements play a part. And sometimes the fish don't bite because it is too hot or too cold or too early or too late.

Yes, even Mr. Walleye has had slow days, but he doesn't hide behind an excuse. The first time we ever fished together, roughly 1970, we never caught what we were after. Instead, he gives the walleyes a little credit.

Walleye anglers all over the country seek Gary's advice. A popular question is: how do you find walleyes? Gary's pat answer is: if the walleyes aren't deep or shallow, they're somewhere in-between.

As for walleye-catching secrets, Roach's secret is that he has none. He works at fishing. I think he can remember almost every

A stringer of crappies with famed angler Gary Roach.

spot he's ever caught a bunch of walleyes. He's a master at boat control. And he's a very patient angler. Most good ones are. With his laid-back style, Roach comes across like some jack pine bumpkin from the back roads of Merrifield, Minnesota, which he is. Still, the walleyes bite for him when they don't bite for the rest of us. And we are left to wonder why.

It's because his fairy tale has come true. He's Mr. Walleye.

Fishing with a Grumpy Old Man

As a fishing companion, Jack Lemmon was far from ordinary. First of all, Lemmon is the most famous ice fisherman in Minnesota, and that's not an easy role to land. Peering into a hole in the ice is not normally a path to movie stardom. In addition, Lemmon is certainly not the first ice angler, nor the last, to have an eye for Ann-Margret. And he's probably not the only fisherman in Minnesota willing to wrestle a fellow angler for possession of a freshly caught walleye.

Drop that fish, Jack. I didn't say that to him, but he would have gotten the joke. Beyond the land of make-believe, Lemmon, the star of *Grumpy Old Men*, does enjoy fishing. He's not avid, not addicted, but he cherishes his angling moments.

"For years, we went to Alaska for salmon," Lemmon said. "We" is Jack and his son Chris, a scriptwriter and actor. The two Lemmons had the chance to sample Minnesota fishing with me during a day off from filming the sequel to *Grumpy* in the Twin Cities. They also were treated to another Minnesota tradition, a walleye shore lunch.

Together in my boat, the screenplay called for catching largemouth bass. The subplot was to catch anything that would bite. Lemmon started casting a white spinnerbait. His son Chris and I tossed plastic worms. "This is great," said Lemmon, basking in the autumn sun. With nary a backlash, Lemmon flicked cast after cast. He said he could handle spinning or baitcaster reels—and it wasn't a throwaway line. Unlike his larger-than-life image on the big screen, Lemmon is a quiet, contemplative angler. A fishing boat is not his stage. He wondered aloud about wood duck houses and admired lakeside homes. "I like it here," he said, complimenting the "nice" Minnesota folk.

The first bass in the boat took a plastic worm. Lemmon stayed with the spinnerbait. The second bass took a purple worm, and the spinnerbait hadn't enticed a swirl. Lemmon wasn't turning grumpy, but he said he'd switch lures. With no previous worm experience, it took him a few practice casts. "Darn, I just had a good hit," he said.

While Lemmon kept casting, he patiently answered the usual fan questions. He doesn't have a favorite movie. He has no interest in retiring. He was raised in the Boston area and first learned to fly-fish for trout in eastern streams. He started fishing as a kid and, when possible, renews his contact with the natural world. He doesn't own a boat but said he intends to change that. "What about those great movie lines: when do you learn the script?" a fishing companion asked. "Usually the night before," Lemmon replied.

We kept on casting. And casting. We hauled in weeds and hooked a few tree branches. Then, a good fish jumped at the end of Chris's fishing line. "What is it?" he shouted. It wasn't the sixty-pound catfish that Lemmon catches in the movie. However, it was Minne-

Jack Lemmon fished with Ron while taking a break from filming the movie Grumpier Old Men.

sota's most notorious piscatorial celebrity: a muskie. "My first muskie, Pops," Chris said.

A few casts later, it was Lemmon's turn as a largemouth bass inhaled the lure. The fish wasn't exactly a wall hanger, a fact that Lemmon jokingly noted. But it was a fish. "It's just great being out here," Lemmon said, his famous face glowing in the afternoon sun. It was a straight line, coming from the heart.

Lemmon's fishing guide wasn't quite as patient. "C'mon bass," the guide said grumpily.

"It's a nice day, anyway," Lemmon countered.

"It's nicer when something's on the end of the line," the grumpy guide said.

Sounded like a movie script.

How I Survived the Sleeper Hold

Gone from memory are the details about how I happened to meet one of my boyhood idols, the champion wrestler Verne Gagne. I do remember that when I was a boy, my father and I watched him wrestle on television. Time after time, our hero Verne would miraculously recover from a severe beating by much larger opponents like that evil Mad Dog Vachon or Larry "The Axe" Hennig. Amazingly, Gagne would eventually win the match, remain the good guy, and maintain his World Champion title. It's no wonder my dad and I always rooted for him.

Verne Gagne's signature wrestling move was something he called the "sleeper hold." Within seconds after he wrapped his arms in strategic areas of an opponent's neck, those human giants would collapse into a heap until the referee held up Gagne's hand in victory. As I got older, I always wondered about that so-called sleeper hold. Just another bit of wrestling showbiz BS?

Decades later, my question about the sleeper hold would be answered. It happened this way. One April in the early 1980s, a group of Minnesota wannabe turkey hunters booked a hunt at my Turkey Track Club camp in the Black Hills. And who should appear? Yes, the legendary Verne Gagne, who turned out to be an enjoyable guest with an easy laugh.

Well, the publicity director of the hunting camp (that be me) called the local newspaper, the *Rapid City Journal*, to give them a scoop: a legend was in town. In short order, a feature writer for the *Journal* drove to our camp in Piedmont, South Dakota, to interview the great Gagne. He was very obliging. For a photograph, the writer suggested that I should stand next to Verne. We were instructed to strike a pose and pretend to be wrestling. To make matters more interesting, I told Verne to put his so-called sleeper hold on me. It would make a great photo. I think I laughed at my own absurd suggestion: sleeper hold, beeper hold, BS hold.

Quickly, Verne Gagne applied his signature sleeper hold. Click went the camera. I think it went click; I wasn't seeing or hearing very straight. Verne released his grip on my neck. I was ready to go . . . down. A few more seconds and I would have been pinned next to the dandelions. I never again pooh-poohed the sleeper hold.

However, I got even—kinda. Some years later, Verne joined his friend, Dr. Jerry Poland, the Crosby, Minnesota, eye doctor, and accepted my invitation to go walleye fishing on Gunisao Lake in Manitoba. It was—and still is—one of the great walleye waters, reachable only by air.

We all had a great morning of fishing and then gathered at noon for a delicious shore lunch of fresh-caught walleyes, a beer or two, and a little bravado. Fishing competition? Oh, Verne Gagne was in He thrived on competition. He turned to me and offered a challenge: "I'll keep up with you fish for fish," he snarled. I accepted and wondered if I should put some money on his stupid challenge. He may be a world champion in the ring, but in the boat he cast like Bozo the Clown. I didn't say that out loud, of course.

Off we went, the champ and me, casting a shoreline loaded with walleyes. Gagne tied on an old Creek Chub plug. Good grief. That Gagne would choose to catch walleyes with a plug that was designed in 1924 to catch anything but walleyes is, well, incredible. Never mind that he actually caught a walleye with it.

"You do not like my choice," he sneered, preparing to apply a bear hug.

"My hero," I replied, "the Creek Chub was a fine lure in its day, but its day ended with the big dance band era."

"Then what do you suggest?" the champ replied.

"I suggest a jig," I said.

Gagne appeared puzzled. "I never have fished with a jig," he said, as he watched me catch yet another walleye.

Twenty minutes later, the score was Verne, three walleyes; me, thirteen walleyes. Verne said my lead wouldn't last long as he was just warming up. Me, I said nothing, just kept casting.

Suddenly I realized my fishing partner wasn't casting, wasn't talking. I looked at the world champ, who was in the bow of the boat, curled in a fetal position and in a state of deep sleep. And then he started snoring. Like a champion. I let him be. Our fishing contest, after all, was just for fun. No money, darn it. An hour or two later, Verne sat up, rubbed his eyes, and quickly asked for the score.

"It's thirty-six to three," I replied. I can't remember if I bragged about whipping the world champ, although I think I mentioned it once or a hundred times around the campfire later that night. Sadly, we never had a fishing rematch, and I never asked again to test the sleeper hold. Verne and I ended in a draw. Not even Mad Dog can say that.

Fishing with the Splendid Splinter

My one and only fishing trip with Ted Williams, the Splendid Splinter, was in the Florida Keys at his beach home in Islamorada. I had been introduced to Ted through former Minnesotans Dick and Carol Knapp. Dick was a fishing guide in the Keys, and Ted liked all fishing guides. He wasn't crazy about talking to the press, but I had special credentials: I wrote about fishing. Plus he liked Minnesotans, he told me.

Williams had many Minnesota connections: he started his career playing baseball for the old Minneapolis Millers; his first wife was from Princeton, and Ted used to do fly rod casting demonstrations at the Northwest Sports Show. Immediately, Ted and I were fishing soul mates. We talked fishing almost constantly. I should say Ted was doing most of the talking. I was simply trying to hang on every word as one might when in the company of an American icon.

One day we sat down for an interview in the comfort of his home. On the wall to my right was a huge oil painting of a gorgeous woman with a bemused expression, as if she was listening while Ted told tarpon-catching stories. Although I was busy taking notes, I occasionally glanced up to admire the painting. It was tastefully done, I had to admit. The lady was completely nude but carefully posed, of course. Finally, I told Ted Williams how much I liked the painting, but did he know the story behind it?

"Oh yes," Ted replied. "That's my wife." Quickly my eyes went back to my notebook. "Beautiful, ain't she?" he added, quickly telling how they met. He sent her a note on an airplane flight asking for a date and signing his name, "Ted." She wrote back, "Ted who?" He had an answer.

Ted's love of fishing was well known. It's been said you only needed to see Ted take one swing to understand his unique hitting talents. The same could be said about his casting skills in a fishing boat. He went after bonefish or tarpon as if they were fastballs down the middle. If he whiffed a cast, if the bonefish spooked, Ted had a line of expletives that would make a prison guard blush.

Ted was supposed to be the guide that day, showing a Minnesota walleye angler (me) how to pitch a perfect cast to a bonefish. I made a few casts, but none with the accuracy that Ted or the bonefish demanded. It might have been my third cast, come to think of it, when Ted said he'd show me how. On the next bonefish, spotted swimming in the shallow flats, Ted's cast with a hooked shrimp for bait landed perfectly in the fish's path. Ted set the hook, and the bonefish made a hundred-yard run as fast as a line drive. A short time later Ted landed the nine-pounder, released it, and immediately removed and replaced the entire spool of line. One spool of line for each fish. Why? There might be a nick in the old line, Ted explained. He wasn't taking any chances on missing the next fish.

Hey, you wouldn't go to the plate with a cracked bat, would you?

For Ted Williams, fishing was not just a pastime. For years he served as a spokesman for Sears fishing tackle, and he took the job seriously. I went along as Ted met with Sears engineers, who were developing a new spinning reel design. "This won't work," he said, looking at the reel's gears. "The drive gear should be like this." Then he'd turn to me, "Isn't that right, Ron?" Do you disagree with a legend?

When Williams died at age eighty-three, the nation mourned the passing of a baseball great. To America's sport fishermen, however, Ted was famous and admired for more than his swing.

Goodbye, Jackpine Bob

Minnesota's Jackpine Bob Cary was laid to rest, and I felt bad about not being there to offer my last respects. Bob was eighty-four years old when he crossed his final portage. I was fortunate to have crossed a few with him over the years.

Yet, if I know Jackpine Bob, he wouldn't give a hoot about me missing his funeral. If he knew I was on a fishing trip, Bob would say fishing is healthier for you than funerals. Truth is, I was on a fishing trip a long distance from Ely, Minnesota, where folks said their last farewells. I'm told it was a big funeral for the size of Ely. The number of mourners would have embarrassed Jackpine. He never viewed himself as anything special, just practical.

Jackpine Bob was one of the state's outdoor legends who fished and hunted and paddled and camped and largely soaked up the meaning of life in northern Minnesota's famed Boundary Waters Canoe Area Wilderness. He was also a talented writer: his last outdoors column in the *Ely Echo* was his own obituary. Bob would say you shouldn't feel sorry for anybody who's fished as much as he has in his life. He said he knew his time was short. He also said he had few regrets.

My regret is I never told Bob Cary how much I admired his wit and wisdom, his outlook on life, and his common sense. *Rain falls in every life, but eventually the sun will shine again. Canoe trips teach that,* he was fond of saying. You don't have to believe that adage. But it's Cary's penchant for yarn-weaving and his commonsense punditry that launched his 1980 campaign for US president as leader of the Fisherman's Party. Cary's political platform called for more fishing time for everybody and a boat in every garage. His fishy campaign even made national news broadcasts. Didn't help, however.

"I suffered one of the worst defeats in history, losing by 63 million votes. I was counting on 60 million votes from fishermen, but I guess they all went fishing on election day," Cary laughed. Is his Fisherman's Party ready for another election year, another campaign? "I'm not running again. Don't want the job. The country's too screwed up." He laughed again. I laughed too. Most of the country laughed as well.

As the years went by, my memorable times with Bob Cary collected like pine pollen on a tent roof. He was a robust paddler who loved to lead an outdoors writer "from the Cities" into the boondocks to one of his favorite haunts, a hot smallmouth bass lake. He said we were going to West Lake. At least, that was Bob's name for the lake. As he promised, the smallmouth action was awesome, one bronze football after another.

Upon my return to the Twin Cities, I looked at a BWCAW map so I would have a visual sense of where Bob and I had caught so many smallmouth. I knew roughly where we portaged out of Basswood and into West. The trouble was: there was no West Lake on the map. I called Jackpine Bob. *Where is West Lake?* He just hooted and hollered. One of Bob's favorite things to do was mess with the minds of city folks who thought their love of wild country made them wilderness experts. Especially if those enthusiasts were outdoor writers.

Sadly, Ol' Jackpine Bob's happy hoots of laughter no longer echo through the pines. In his obituary, Bob wrote he was somewhat curious as to what lies ahead. Perhaps another great adventure, he wondered.

To West Lake, no doubt.

The Damnedest Fish Story Ever

In the quiet of their Minnesota country home, Bob and Snookie Ploeger could sit in front of their television set and, time and again, watch that awful moment. Roll the videotape.

See Bob Ploeger's bended fishing rod. . . . See the huge salmon hooked in Alaska's Kenai River. . . . Watch the landing nets scoop and come up empty. . . . Hear the river guide's shout of despair. . . . Bob Ploeger says nothing. Feel the silence of defeat.

A visitor is tempted to watch that fishing moment unfold again. Okay, one more time. Maybe the outcome will change. Roll the tape.

So begins a classic fishing story of our times. A classic? When there's a thirty-seven-hour fight between angler and fish, the story is a classic. Yah, thirty-seven hours. Consecutive.

Starring a quiet, devout Minnesotan, Bob Ploeger, who at the age of sixty-three found himself in a modern-day version of Ernest Hemingway's epic *The Old Man and the Sea*. However, there is one difference. The fish on Ploeger's line wasn't fiction. It was a giant king salmon. It was so huge and Ploeger fought the giant for so many hours, the battle was recorded by Anchorage television news crews, reported on live radio from the riverbanks, and carried on the wires to the nation's newspapers. Witnesses suspected the salmon was a possible new world hook-and-line record, a legendary hundred-pounder. Anxiously, all of Alaska waited for Ploeger to subdue the giant.

Imagine the drama. The stress. The adrenaline rush. If fighting a big fish for ten minutes is gut-wrenching, try thirty-seven hours.

The fishing adventure started routinely enough. Not much biting. Then, at about 12:30 in the afternoon, Ploeger was having lunch when he felt a strike on the line. He set the hook—twice, in fact—but the big fish didn't move much for two hours. For the same two hours, Ploeger's guide kept the drift boat near the fish in the swift current of the Kenai.

Suddenly, the fish decided to move—in a hurry downstream. Ploeger's thirty-pound test line was about to be tested. The fish stopped again. Time went by. Lots of time.

Next, the salmon moved back up the river, swimming into some short rapids, beyond the path of the drift boat. Ploeger had to jump to a different boat with another guide and outboard power. Snookie agreed to stay behind with the other boat. The fish fight went on. The salmon started moving downstream again, this time four miles. Still, nobody had seen the fish.

Four hours after hooking the fish, Ploeger and the guides finally got a good look at the end of the line. Oh, goodness. The king salmon appeared to be five feet long with a really big belly. The fish showed no signs of getting tired.

Time went on. The sun went down. The boat's gas tank was nearing empty. Ploeger and his guides were hungry and tired. Six more hours would pass before they'd see the salmon a second time, when it surfaced momentarily. Most of the time, the huge fish simply hugged the bottom like a rock. From midnight to about 5:30 AM the salmon hadn't moved 150 yards.

Dawn arrived. Thursday. Snookie and others showed up on another boat with breakfast, an egg McMuffin with sausage from Soldotna. Like her husband, she also was without sleep.

By late afternoon, a local radio station had begun to broadcast riverside updates. Television news cameras showed up alongside Ploeger's boat. Spectators—a crowd of 250 or more—gathered to watch. Crowd or not, Ploeger also had a bladder problem. Two television reporters volunteered to "stand around" while he kneeled in the boat, his one hand on the fishing pole. A guide held the urine bottle.

In one stretch of time Ploeger had been holding the fishing rod for seventeen straight hours without a short rest. Exhaustion was coming. By midnight of the second night, Ploeger was unsure if he really wanted to break the record. He also was concerned about the guide's fee, since his eight-hour, two-hundred-dollar trip was well into overtime. And they had consumed almost forty-five gallons of gasoline to stay with the fish. The guide told Ploeger he would charge for only one day. Ploeger also prayed: "Lord, it's your will."

And then it happened. At 1:30 AM on Friday—thirty-seven hours since Ploeger and the fish connected—the salmon moved into shallow water against the riverbank. Quickly, Ploeger and his two guides made a major decision: they would attempt to net the long salmon, using two landing nets that were three to four feet wide. Amazingly, the TV crews were still there; the camera lights were on. The giant fish was now in plain view and still hooked. In unison, the guides reached with their landing nets. The battle was over.

Snookie cried, "Oh, no." Nobody else said a word. The two guides—tears streaming down their faces—slumped into the boat seats. Ploeger tapped his guide's shoulder and murmured, "It's okay." The salmon was gone.

The Ploegers slept for ten hours and then started the trip back to Minnesota. When they arrived home, neighbors jokingly had left a can of salmon on the kitchen table.

As every angler knows, in every lost fish, there's a little pain. Some of the agony is short-lived; other lost fish memories hurt forever. While I sat in Bob Ploeger's kitchen, asking him to retell his salmon story, he paused. "The Lord knew I wanted it," Ploeger said, fighting back a tear. "I guess the Lord is for catch and release."

Poetic Opening Day

When Minnesota's snowbanks begin to melt, aided by warming breezes from the south, most of us come down with a case of spring fever. Is this merely March deception or a cruel April?

Probably. But it matters not. It's never wrong to start thinking about fishing for spring crappies, opening the cabin, restoring the dock, planning for the walleye opener—thoughts that annually flood our minds as the snow melts. At least my mind.

To make matters worse, I happened upon an aged book, *Poems of Our Great Outdoors*, written by B. H. "Red" Fisher. It's out of print now, last published by an outboard maker, Mercury.

> When'ya feel let down, just short of your goal.
> And you'd like to hide or crawl in a hole.
> Well here's a prescription to rest your soul.
> A boat, a lake, and a stout fishing pole.

I'd never met the man, but Red Fisher's fame long ago had spread from his Canada homeland into Minnesota. Until his death, Fisher was a Canadian legend, known for his grassroots humor and practical approaches to life itself. His fame was spread via newspaper columns and a television series, the *Red Fisher Show*, which aired across Canada.

> When'ya think for sure you'll lose your mind,
> In the fall when your job seems so unkind.
> Here's one tip I know will make you unwind.
> Get a boat, a lake, some ducks and a blind.

Unfortunately, the folks who knew or remember Red Fisher also are slowly diminishing in number, including the late Bill Fontana of Fort Frances, Ontario. Actually, Fontana was a legend of his own, a famed logroller with his logrolling dogs. He appeared at dozens of Northwest Sports Shows in Minneapolis. And hundreds of Minnesotans rented Fontana's houseboats on scenic Rainy Lake before he sold the business. Fontana mailed his copy of Fisher's book to me with a note: the poems "might have been written long ago but they still have meaning."

Just what do you do, when your motor quits,
And you're drifting downstream, towards that roar,
You left the oars by the barbecue pits,
And your wife left the gas on the shore.

Just what do we do, when the chips are down,
And we can't find an answer, worth while,
I guess it don't help, to grumble and frown,
So we might as well face it, and SMILE.

Fisher wrote about the life and times, the heart and soul of being an outdoor person. He also pondered how the advance of modern comforts might gradually erode our connections to the earth. About flying he once wrote:

We move so fast we're missing
All the wonders and the worth
Of nature softly kissing,
All the wildlife on the earth.

Huge mountains pass like pebbles.
Great lakes, like limpid pools.
For speed has made us rebels,
And reactionary fools.

Humor is a common outdoor bond that didn't go unnoticed in Fisher's verses. He was fond of boats, especially boats of speed, and Fisher couldn't understand anybody who didn't likewise appreciate them. A couple of excerpts from "Boats":

There comes a time in each man's life,
That makes his past remote.
And, friend, that time's in store for you,
When you first run a boat.

So now, let's weigh the pros and cons.
Then pity all the dotes,
Who keep on doing something else,
Instead of running boats.

Fisher's most critical verse was inevitably aimed at despoilers and polluters and, lastly, at humankind's own stupidity toward natural resources.

What species is there here on earth,
Who'll soon pollute their right of birth,
Who'll blight their woodlands, lakes and skies,
Who'll kill what swims, crawls, runs or flies?

What mammals choose to go astray,
From nature's everlasting way?
Whose very population zoom,
Is slowly spelling out their doom?

But life goes on. And so do fishing openers, as Fisher penned "'Twas the Night Before Fishing":

'Twas the night before fishing,
When toast after toast,
Finally left no one sober,
Not even the host.
The whole camp was in turmoil,
The gear was piled deep.
And the dishes from dinner
Were stacked in a heap.

And the poker chips jingled.
And the cards flashed bright,
To the bleary eyed players,
Glued there for the night.
Course the stories were flying,
Complete with damned lies.

Like the fish that Jake mentioned
He landed on flies.

Or the sexy achievement
Slim made with that Chick.
That he savorly bragged of
With "hic" after "hic."
Like the one when Mike scrubbed out
Results of that scare.
When he ran to the outhouse
And into a bear.

Or the one of the musky,
Max told with a gloat.
That leaped high for his spinner,
And fell in the boat.
Yes the stories were flying,
The gang was unwound.
As their pent up emotions,
Spilled out all around.

Then a loon called out loudly,
From far in the lake.
And in sudden awareness,
It jarred us awake.
Each man of us now knew it
Was time to turn in.
For tomorrow we'd battle
The surge of the fin.

Just the stillness of darkness,
Remained to make clear.
'Twas the night before fishing
For another long year.

Thanks, Red, for reminding us.

HUNTIN' DOGS AND ME

No Such Thing as a Free Dog

The first hunting dog I ever owned cost me twenty bucks. That's not a large amount of money unless you're twelve years old, which I was. My first dog meant going into debt. Little did I know, decades later, I'd still be making doggie payments. No matter what the newspaper ads say, free or cheap puppies and dogs are like free lunches. There's no such thing.

My own venture into dog debt began with Taffy, a light blonde Cocker Spaniel with a great nose for birds, cockleburs, and rolling in fresh cow pies. Despite her cow-pasture wandering, Taffy could do no wrong in my young eyes. She was always full of surprises. Sometimes she'd even come when called.

Taffy was really a birdy dog too. If she smelled the scent of a pheasant, hot or cold, she'd follow that bird to the next county—and often did. Taffy and I would have brought home a lot of pheasants if I could have run a little faster. Thanks to Taffy, I saw lots of birds out of range. Probably just as well. If pheasants had been close, I'd have probably missed anyway.

To paraphrase W. C. Fields, there's never a hunting dog so bad that it can't serve as a good example. This adage reminds me of a black Lab named Fancy.

Fancy belonged to my friend Bob, who eventually realized that as a hunting dog, Fancy was anything but. You could say Fancy was unique: a retriever who hated to retrieve. All of which explains why one morning on the Canadian prairies, as Bob and I were about to go duck hunting, Bob decided to leave Fancy in the motel room. We would use my Lab, Coot, a retriever who at least would retrieve.

I was particularly overjoyed by the decision. It was the best and easiest choice to make to prevent heartburn. And I knew Bob was relieved too.

Fancy loved to sleep in Bob's bed. We also knew that, as a laid-back dog, Fancy wouldn't bother the maid when she came to clean the room. However, as it turned out, the maid didn't even try to make the bed or open the curtains. For one thing, when the maid entered the room she couldn't find the drapes. Well, not right away.

Fancy must have torn down the curtains so she could see Bob leave. We can only guess why she wanted to dig through the mattress and scatter most of it on the floor. I guess Fancy thought she could dig her way out to find Bob. She was as far as the bedsprings when the maid knocked.

When we returned from duck hunting, we should have known something was wrong. It was still early, yet everybody was up, including the motel manager, who was waiting to greet us. We thought he wanted to see our ducks. But when he started talking to Bob, his teeth and lips barely moved. His nose was gasping like a gauge on a pressure cooker. Obviously, the task of managing a motel had finally shattered his nerves. When he pointed at Fancy, his body quivered and his hands shook, poor fella.

To Bob's credit, he apologized for everything Fancy did, including the fit of loud barking that began just before sunrise. Bob didn't argue over the three-hundred-dollar bill, either. Oh, he could have protested the drape charges, I suppose. Actually, Fancy had shredded only one pair of drapes, leaving the other curtain somewhat messy but easily cleaned. Certainly the manager wasn't exaggerating over the condition of the mattress. On that, Bob agreed. Its twin size had been halved by a gaping hole. The motel door also was damaged, although Bob said it's amazing how teeth and claw marks will disappear with a little sandpaper and wood filler. Bob settled up with the motel manager, who was still rather irritable when he said, *don't come back.*

Aah yes, no dogs are perfect. I've had my share.

For example, I'll never forget the day a Brittany puppy I had ordered showed up at the house. I had bought the pup sight unseen from a professional dog trainer. It was the cutest little black puppy. Black puppy? Wait: Brittany puppies aren't supposed to have black coats. While my daughters kissed and hugged the pup, I frantically called the trainer. He said the pup was "a little dark" but should lighten up as it got older. If not, he said, I could bring the pup back and get a Brittany that actually looked like a Brittany.

One day later it was too late to think of exchanging pups. My daughters had developed an ironlike attachment to the pup, naming her Kelly. 'Twas a fine pet, Kelly was. However, three dog trainers tried in vain to make Kelly, the black Brittany, act like a Brittany. Birds in the air? Kelly didn't care. Was she curious about a dead pheasant in the grass? Not a bit. Garbage? Well, that's another story . . .

Why Dogs Do What?

Finally it can be written. Finally we humans are free to ponder aloud those most delicate, sometimes embarrassing moments of being a dog owner. Our guilt has been washed away by a fella named Tom Davis, author of a book entitled *Why Dogs Do That*.

I am relieved. If I could meet a certain lady again I would apologize profusely and explain what the hell my dog was doing. It all began innocently enough. One day a woman showed up unannounced at the front door and kindly rang the doorbell. Was she a long-lost relative perhaps? Was she selling something?

I opened the door. She walked in. Before I could ask her name or what she wanted, my black Labrador, Raven, charged at the woman and, with wagging tail, abruptly poked her cold nose between the lady's thighs.

The woman was not expecting this. Me either. I could feel my face turning red as if I had overindulged with cheap wine. I pretended not to see Raven's ill-mannered nose posture but assured the lady that the dog was just being very friendly and was curious about anybody who comes to the house. Quickly the frowning woman—expecting another poke of the nose from Raven—turned to guard her crotch. "Heel," I shouted.

What was my dog doing? Now, thanks to *Why Dogs Do That* I know that Raven was merely checking the lady's identity. Dogs use their nose for this task. Let's be blunt. Dogs sniff the rear end of other dogs for the same reason, to kinda get to know them. It's the canine version of "Hi, who are you?" While dogs may not understand things like human perfumes, Davis says dogs recognize other dogs by their "signature" scent. One sniff also answers the question of male or female. In other words, Raven was only wondering if the lady was a member of the pack.

Now on to more pleasant canine behaviors. Does your dog sleep in bed with you? Of course. If you were a dog would you choose the floor or a warm, soft mattress? However, there may be more to this bedroom ploy. "In the context of the pack dynamic, the dog that's allowed to sleep with the alpha male and/or female feels as if it has climbed another rung on the social ladder," Davis writes.

What about this strange habit of your dog eating grass? My dad used to say it was a sign that the weather was going to change. Not so, Davis explains: "Dogs are carnivores by nature but omnivores by necessity." He said dogs not only enjoy the taste of fresh greens but also evolved as predators who ate the paunch and innards of prey, including vegetation in various stages of digestion. Oh, great. However, a dog's stomach isn't well equipped to digest fresh grass, which explains why the family pet will eagerly eat grass only to upchuck it all minutes later. Apparently a dog with an upset stomach will eat grass specifically to induce vomiting.

Doggy questions are many, of course: Why do retrievers retrieve? Why do dogs chase cars? Why do dogs beg for food? Why do dogs eat cow pies? Why do males lift their legs but females squat?

Perhaps you've noticed that a dog often turns in a circle before lying down? Davis says this behavior is missing a scientific explanation. According to folklore, dogs turn in a circle to flush any snakes away. Probably not true. Davis says the turning began with a dog's close relatives, wolves, who circle in order to flatten the grass and make a comfortable bed.

Lastly, dog owners need to know that their canine pet will try to practice an X-rated act on occasion. That is, your dog may try to hump your leg at the most inopportune times. If this humping act occurs during a meeting of your book club, please remain calm. Simply push the dog away, smile at your guests, and explain that Fido is just practicing. Good dog, Fido.

Coot, the Wonder Dog

After a recent spasm of soul-searching, I feel compelled to reveal the truth about my dog Coot, the black Lab whose hunting prowess I often featured in my bird hunting adventures. Consider this a posthumous confession, so to speak.

It begins when Coot had disappeared from my yard at nightfall and was still missing shortly before midnight. Given the time passed, Coot's affection for strangers, and his lack of experience with speeding cars, I seriously doubted his return.

If our hunting days were over, I mused, his reputation ought to go with him. Everybody is proud of their own dog, which means we overlook shortcomings and accidents on the new rug. And I'm no different. Coot has romped with me from the duck prairies of Canada to the pheasant cornfields of Iowa. He would grudgingly fetch woodcock even though he disliked their scent and loose feathers. On snow-swept duck passes, Coot has shivered while I shivered too. Chilled or not, Coot always was ready for the next retrieve in icy water. And if we marched all day in the grouse-less forests, Coot would simply harass chipmunks to pass the time.

Let there be no doubt, he liked to go hunting. Just pick up a shotgun. Never mattered what time of year. He'd be the first thing in the truck. For seven years we shared the fortunes and failings of being afield; many of those forays went public. And many of you have since inquired, "How's Coot?" And I'd always reply, "Fine, just fine."

Well, that was a lie.

Coot was a four-legged dingbat. Sometimes nuts, I swear. He'd be unhappy in the backyard kennel. And I'd be unhappy when he was out. He'd scare kids, neighbors, and joggers. Not because he'd bite or even growl. Rather, he'd bowl—bowl people over with enthusiasm. He wouldn't jump up on me with dirty paws because I'd trained him not to jump up. So he'd leap on other people.

Coot's greatest sin was he wouldn't mind the wife. Never did listen to her. Many times she'd been prompted to request an eviction notice: Coot's or mine. Coot was trained to go straight to the kennel on command. When the wife so ordered, with her finest screaming voice, Coot always took the long way, passing through the garden, at the same speed trees grow. Worse, he'd learned not to listen to me either. I'd say, "Sit and stay." He'd stop and wait. And move when he thought it was safe.

Immediately out of the kennel, he'd be a streaking gob of black fur with a high-strung garden hose and a full bladder. Every tree, bush, or flower needed dousing. Some are still living. Coot's next stop was the kitchen patio door in search of table scraps. Down in St. Louis, the Purina folks have employed dieticians, veterinarians, physiologists, and a slick advertising agency to produce a dog food so well balanced that all you add is love. Coot preferred last week's tuna casserole. His fondness for Purina or any other commercial dog food ranked slightly ahead of starvation. Of course, this assessment did not apply to the high-priced mush sold in cans. After inhaling everything on the patio (including dry pieces of bread crust intended for the birds), Coot's next ploy was to plan an avenue of escape. Time and again he'd been caught and punished for leaving the yard. I tried training, cursing, and flogging. I sought counseling from Coot's vet, Dr. Norb Epping.

"Sometimes it's impossible to keep a dog home, particularly a male," he advised. I inquired about castration. The idea was tabled. "Let's try a light tranquilizer," Epping suggested. That worked the first day. After that Coot developed an immunity. "You know," said Epping, "if you were in a kennel all day, you'd probably act that way too." I agreed with that premise. But I'm also fairly convinced that after tearing around the house and garden forty times I'd want to slow down. Coot didn't.

Thus confronted with growing impatience around the neighborhood plus fragile tranquility in the household, I decided to experiment. If Coot wasn't kept in the kennel, I surmised, perhaps he wouldn't be so rambunctious and bent on tearing up the yard and leaving for the next township. He'd become content to be free in the yard, wouldn't he?

Coot was gone forty-five minutes later. Well, good riddance.

Who needs a dog like that? Yes, we've had some fine times together. But there are other dogs that enjoy hunting and staying home.

Coot was gone. So why write some big tearjerker story and give the impression I'd just lost the greatest of all canine companions? Coot was a pain. And you know where.

Danged if he wasn't back in his kennel the next morning.

The Day Kyla Died

As the days cool and the leaves begin to fall, there is something in the air that is not seen; it is felt. Most of us who hunt know when it happens, although the source remains a mystery. Maybe it's the chill in the morning air. Or the changing autumn landscape. Or the fall shuffle of wild animals that matches an inner clock of my own species. All I know is I feel it.

Kyla, my black Lab, could smell it, I swear. The message was the same: it was time to go hunting. Nothing else explains Kyla's sudden left turn out of the kennel that day when I opened the door. After days, weeks, and months of turning right and running to her usual "go potty" spot, Kyla charged to her left for a quick sniff at the back door of my truck. She bounded back to me and yipped once. She could smell it.

The back of the truck was loaded with her portable kennel and my hunting clothes, ammo, and shotgun. Her nose told her. It was opening day of Minnesota's pheasant season. It was also our eleventh October as hunting companions.

When we roamed the pheasant haunts together, Kyla's tail always said what she couldn't: birds had been there or still were. Sometimes, despite hours of fruitless hunting, her tail said she wasn't quitting. Kyla wore her heart on the end of her tail. Most hunting dogs do.

This sense of teamwork makes the hunter-dog bond strong. Of course, there are good hunting dogs and some not so good. We've hunted with both. But every hunting dog is worth braggin' and boastin' about a little, at least. Why? Because together you've clogged through the same marsh muck, shivered in the same cold, and thirsted in the same heat. Together you've watched the same sunrises and shared the same sandwiches. And your hearts—hunter and dog—have fluttered with the same gaudy ringnecks.

Kyla was always good company. She knew when to be quiet in the car during long drives to pheasant country. She knew it didn't pay to whine with anticipation until the roads turned to gravel or worse. She was, in fact, one of the best hunting dogs to ever heel at my side. Forgive me for bragging, but she was all a retriever should be, with a good nose and a willingness to fetch forever. Kyla also did what most retrievers don't do: she pointed—stiff as a statue—if the bird held tight.

Oh, Kyla wasn't perfect, of course. She never came into season, so she could never have puppies. She knew one sharp blast of the whistle meant "sit," but sometimes she didn't hear it. Sometimes she forgot who was in charge. Still, she was close to perfect.

One late October, Kyla and I headed to South Dakota to what can be the utopia of bird land. On the first afternoon west of Redfield, Kyla rousted three ringnecks and I took three shots for our three-bird limit. What a team.

It should be noted that we also were hunting slower and easier. Neither of us was as young as we used to be. At the age of ten and a half, Kyla had a muzzle streaked gray and her pace was that of an elderly canine.

In the glow of our successful first-day hunt together, I silently wondered if this year might be Kyla's last as a member of the team. Even the thought of it was painful. Last year or not, we would hunt again tomorrow, I comforted myself.

The next afternoon, Kyla and I joined up with other hunters to walk a vast field of tall prairie grass near Pierre, South Dakota. The day was unseasonably hot. Kyla was ready to go, as always. Within the first two hundred yards, a flock of pheasants—eight or more— burst into the air. Shotguns fired. A ringneck dropped. Kyla raced to the bird and brought it to me.

Already she was panting from the heat and excitement. We resumed hunting. Twenty-five minutes later, Kyla's panting had turned to a heavy heaving of her lungs. I offered her water. She refused.

Next, she no longer quartered in front. Instead, she walked behind me. Then suddenly, she quit walking at all. I called for help. We lifted Kyla onto the back end of a pickup and rushed her to a farm pond. I laid her half in and half out of the water to cool off. Gradually, her panting slowed. She tried to walk, but her back legs were paralyzed. Heatstroke? Heart attack? I had no idea. Later, Kyla's veterinarian, Dr. Norb Epping, told me she could have suffered both as the symptoms are classic.

Several hours later, Kyla seemed to be recovering. We had taken a shower together. She was dried off and was lying upright in our motel room, her eyes watching my every move.

"You gonna be okay?" I said. I looked at Kyla's tail for her answer. The tail didn't move.

Sometime in the night, I sensed that Kyla was lying on the floor next to my bed. I reached down to pet her. Then I knew. Kyla was dead.

"Kyla went the way she would have wanted to go, hunting," Dr. Epping said.

Yes, but the rest of the team is left with a broken heart.

Three Ravens, Forever Loved

This doggy story is a tough one to write. How do you explain a phenomenon with a shiny black coat, a wagging tail, and a Labrador personality? Where do you begin? How did a good but normal bird hunting dog become one of the best-known canines in Minnesota, if not much of America? You mean the Lab wearing the red bandana? The dog we see on television? Yah, that dog.

Let's start at the beginning. As a bird hunter, I've had a hunting dog companion for decades. Raven was not the first. The first was a bird Cocker Spaniel, Taffy, who rousted pheasants with gusto, most of them out of shotgun range. Later on, my canine partners included golden retrievers also birdy and anxious to please. One day I was offered a tall, male black Lab with the promise he was a retrieving fool and could compete in field trials. I named him Peg. Oh, he loved to fetch, but he often wasn't smart about it. Maybe the fault was with his trainer (me).

More years passed and more Labs touched my heart, most leaving good memories. Then, in 1994, along came a black Lab puppy from a friend, dog trainer Tom Dokken. She seemed smart. Black birds like ravens are smart too, I thought. I named her Raven.

A first "real" hunt with a pup is like no other. Raven's was no different. And I shan't bore you with the details. It's just a little thing, and it means more to me than to you, I suspect.

That is, unless you know the meaning of starting over. For me, starting over began months earlier when Kyla, my black Lab, died of a heatstroke on a South Dakota pheasant hunt in late October. She was ten years old. In some ways, my heartbreak continued even after Raven moved into our home. You know seven-week-old puppies: untrained, unruly. Her first week with us will be remembered for a month's supply of yesterday's newspapers on the floor and tireless yipping in the wee hours of the night. It didn't get any easier when she missed the newspaper.

Oh, there were moments of joy. Raven was a lovable pup (aren't they all?) who soon took to fetching old socks and stalking imaginary prey behind the couch. Slowly, we began the bonding process that would eventually link us across countless pheasant fields and duck sloughs.

At the age of five months, Raven was ready to discover the meaning of gunfire and to chase real birds with beating wings. Pro trainer Tom Dokken assisted with the introductions, using barn pigeons and live ammo. Right before our eyes, an amazing transition unfolded. Raven began discovering and following her instincts, instilled over centuries of bird hunting DNA passed on by relatives unknown.

The first Raven, 1995.

In my backyard, Raven's game was mostly about fetching. She fetched in the yard, in the water, in the tall grass. She learned whistle commands, like "come" and "sit." She learned there was no part of "no" she could ignore. Yet, little by little, she showed me her heart. Thus, we began a new journey. In the seasons ahead, she'd learn about the wily ways of ringnecks. And I would learn her signals with a thumping tail and anxious movements in pheasant habitat.

That's what starting over is all about. It's not always a task one wants to do. Sometimes there is the pain of losing the old dog, but then your heart mends and, funny thing, your old legs begin to feel younger too.

Since the first, there have been two more Ravens, mothers and daughters—all wonderful hunters. And each, in her own time, was "the star of the show" on *Minnesota Bound* on KARE-TV, the NBC affiliate, as well as on early shows on ESPN2, the Outdoor Channel, and Fox Sports North.

The first appearance of Raven I, on the first *Minnesota Bound* program, happened completely by accident. My lovely wife, Denise, suggested that Raven sit next to me. My cameraman, Joe Harewicz, asked for "something bright or colorful" for the dog to wear. *What could that be?* I wondered. I didn't normally dress up my hunting dogs. I walked down the hall and there—hanging on a coatrack— was a red bandana. The cameraman said, "Perfect." In that moment, Raven became the best-dressed star of the show. And the rest is history. Ravens would wear the bandana for the next twenty-four years.

How did a red bandana happen to be on the coatrack? To this day, I have no idea. My guess? I think God put it there.

Last Hunt with Raven

Raven, my black Lab, was lying stretched out on the living room floor the other day. Her back legs were twitching, and she whimpered softly. She seemed to be dreaming, if that's what dogs do. Gene Hill once wrote, "Our greatest [hunting] trophies are not things, but times." Perhaps hunting dogs feel the same way; perhaps they dream of great times afield in autumns gone by. We can only hope.

This much I know: our times together, Raven and me, are winding down to a precious few. This autumn, she has become an old dog and, for the first time, at the age of eleven, is older than me in dog years. I'm not sure when her aging body became so obvious. Months ago, she started limping a little on her right front leg. Her back hips seemed weaker too. The vet's diagnosis was arthritis. *Comes with age*, he said. I nodded, having a little arthritis myself. "Give her Rimadyl," the doc said. "It'll help. Without it, she'd be crippled."

Steve Reider once observed that when you get a puppy, "you're about to embark on an adventure, which will create memories that no one can ever take from you." If you've ever followed your dog through the pheasant fields or grouse trails, you know what Reider was writing about. All of us who go afield with hunting dogs have our own doggy adventures and fond memories.

Raven was born in my garage and, at age six months, was the third Raven to gain fame as "the star of the *Minnesota Bound* television show." She was a natural in front of the camera. What most television viewers never knew about this canine celebrity is she also starred as a retriever of anything with feathers. Excuse me for boasting.

Memories with Raven? I've got a bunch. But you know what? You always want more. Okay, one more—maybe? *Do we do more bird hunting this fall? Do we not? She's old. Is it over? Am I being selfish to ask an old dog to retrieve one more pheasant?* Answers don't come easily. She seems so content just hanging out, sleeping in comfort, eating on schedule, taking her Rimadyl. Of course, I never asked Raven what she wanted. I just assumed. After all, her interest in catching a Frisbee went away months ago.

The other day I walked out of the basement adorned in hunting clothes and carrying a cased 12 gauge. Raven raised her head. She started for the door. I'd been busted. She was not about to be left behind. She knew. And I knew. *Can't do this*, I said to myself, tears swelling in my eyes. My wife asked if something was wrong. "No," I said, lying. "I changed my mind; she's coming along." It was quickly obvious: her body was old, but her hunting heart was forever young. *We'll take it easy in the field*, I said to myself.

"Hunt 'em up," I ordered. Just like the days of old. For the first fifteen minutes or so, I was watching a veteran Raven in her prime checking out corn rows and other ringneck haunts. She rousted a bird. I fired. She retrieved. Just like the days of old. She would have had more retrieves, but younger Labs got to the birds first. She seemed resigned to the fact her competitive fetching days were behind.

Gradually, however, her pace slowed. It was time for a break. Raven didn't seem to mind. I lifted her into the car kennel. She flopped down on the cushion and let out a low groan. We had one more memory together.

As I write this, Raven is in her favorite place—in the house, on the floor, next to me. Neither of us knows how much hunting time we still have to share. Will Rogers once noted, "If there are no dogs in heaven, then when I die I want to go where they went."

Guess I'm headed for a field of pheasants.

Raven's Story Ends

The "star of the show"—Raven, the Third—has left her hay bale. She went quietly and peacefully in the night while Native American flute music played until the light faded from her eyes. She was an old Labrador, almost fourteen years of age, who outlived her grandmother and her mother.

It's been said you get only one good dog in your life. Not true. I've had many wonderful dogs, including three Ravens who excelled at rousting ringnecks on camera from Kansas to Minnesota. Gene Hill once wrote, "While it's important to have a good dog to hunt over, it's more important to have a good dog to be with." All three Ravens fit both categories. All were special to me. What's more, the Ravens also were special to you. Wherever she appeared—boat shows, car shows, Game Fair, state fair—you could not resist a pat on her head. And Raven could not resist a wag of her tail. You knew her name; you asked where she was. She was your "star of the show" too. It was a phenomenon, and to this day I can't explain it.

Sign on a theater in Austin, Minnesota, when Ron was an evening speaker— with Raven, of course.

As I grieve my own loss, I don't pretend to speak for the joy and sorrow you've experienced with your own canine companions, past and present. However, we share the same emotions—the joy of a puppy; the heartache of losing a family member.

Life without Raven will go on as it must. Some folks ask, "Will you get another Labrador retriever in the future?" My answer is: *It's doubtful but . . . maybe.* As someone once said, dogs leave paw prints on your heart. So now the sadness subsides, leaving the good times behind as you think about your dog and you. Mark Twain offered an honest reflection: "Heaven goes by favor," he wrote, "if [heaven] went by merit, you would stay out and your dog would go in."

When to Say Goodbye

Saying goodbye to your dog—oh, what a heartrending, gut-wrenching experience it is. Most likely many of you have had such a moment, and you know the pain. Meanwhile, those who haven't but who still have a dog to love will often find themselves looking ahead with regret or even fear for when their time comes to say goodbye. We also know the death of a loved member of a family, human or animal, is a grievous moment, differentiated only by the depth of a heavy heart. In either case, the pain is inescapable. Nothing that I may write will eliminate certain despair when it's time to say goodbye.

When my dog Raven, the original television star, died, my depth of sadness was beyond belief. She played a huge role in my television career. While my intentions are not to rekindle that sad memory, sharing the painful process might be helpful for those of you whose final day with Fido will surely arrive. As I reflect on the Labrador retrievers that have brightened my life, the least painful goodbyes were those that required nothing from me but a very heavy heart.

Coot, a male, was ten years old and stricken with cancer. When the day came to say goodbye, Coot was in the basement, refusing to touch his favorite treat. I called the vet. "I'm bringing Coot," I sobbed. I dreaded the next step, loading Coot into the truck. He loved being in the truck. It meant we were going to do something fun, go fetch stuff or go bird hunting. This ride in the truck wouldn't be for fun, and I was glad Coot didn't know it. Or did he?

When I returned to the basement to get Coot for his last ride, I was in for a surprise. Coot spared me. He was already dead.

Kyla was the next doggy love of my life, a black Lab who pointed ringnecks like, well, like a pointer. On a hot October day in South Dakota, Kyla flushed a dozen ringnecks from one spot. Shotguns fired; hunters yelled; birds fell. Kyla rushed to do what retrievers do. She was ten years old and knew the routine. Quickly, Kyla searched for downed birds and fetched those she found. Suddenly, before I could say, "Good dog," her energy faded, her panting turned heavy and laborious, and her breathing became desperate. She fell to the ground. She refused water. What I didn't know: Kyla was having a heatstroke. She died a few hours later.

Soon after, Raven, the original, came into my life. I also knew that twice—with Coot and with Kyla—I had avoided the ultimate agony, the decision to "put down the dog." (More kindly we like to say "putting the dog to sleep." Let's be honest. You don't bawl your eyes out over a dog that's going to sleep.) Over the years, this un-wanted moment, this dreaded decision came up in conversations with Raven's veterinarians, Drs. Norb and Jay Epping, from the Blaine Area Pet Hospital. *How do you know when the time has come? How can you be sure it's the right thing to do?* Your head spins. The questions are many. Your answer is final.

Dr. Jay Epping said a dog will often tell you that the time has come. Raven had quit eating and drinking. Dr. Norb Epping said if you come to realize your dog isn't enjoying life anymore, maybe that's the time to say goodbye. Raven's tail had quit wagging.

I peered into Raven's old and sad eyes. There was no glimmer of hope. She was twelve years old; there was no turning back the clock. Yet, was this the right thing to do? To keep her alive and spare my pain would be a selfish thing. No, the dog you love deserves dig-nity. "It's time," I cried. Dr. Epping agreed.

The time had come to say goodbye.

A-HUNTING WE WILL GO

Don't Be Late

For some time now (since the sixth century), we've been told there are seven deadly sins we should avoid. Pope Gregory I, also known as St. Gregory the Great, is credited with the original list. I shall refrain from listing the seven sins for fear many readers, including this writer, may have to confess to all seven. Instead, I'm suggesting today that one more sin be added for a new total of eight deadly sins. I discovered the eighth sin following a series of mornings in pursuit of a Minnesota wild turkey.

The sin revelation began like this: One morning while driving to my turkey hunting ground, I rounded a bend in the road and there on the roadside was a huge tom in a strutting, courtship frame of mind while in the presence of a female turkey. At that moment I realized I had committed the eighth sin. Tardy. Not on time. By any name, I was late to the woods. In turkey hunting, there is no greater sin. Oh, I know you can kill turkeys at midmorning, high noon, or late afternoon. However, the hour before sunrise is best. It's the time when savvy turkey hunters are in their seat at the base of a tree.

Thinking back, I can't remember being late to chase turkeys beyond a few minor exceptions, such as too many nightcaps. Fact is, when I was a squirrel hunting teenager, I was never late to the woods. Squirrels are active at sunrise; they show themselves. I knew this because I was the Best Squirrel Hunter in Allamakee County, Iowa—a title I bestowed on myself but with which nobody ever argued, so I kept it.

Upholding this title also meant I couldn't ever be late. To be late is to sin. A few years ago on opening day of the deer season I was crossing a small frozen creek when the ice broke and water filled one of my Sorel boots. It was the right foot as I recall. Rather than turn around and go back to camp for dry boots and socks, I trudged on, believing my foot would be warm for awhile yet, anyway. When I reached my deer stand, my right foot was feeling a little numb but tolerable. Ten minutes later, a small buck walked in and didn't walk away. Quickly, I field dressed the deer and hustled back toward camp with one good foot and one totally numb foot. I'd fetch the deer later.

The moral of the story? Frozen toes is no reason to be late.

On the subject of turkey hunting, sin number eight is especially grievous because ninety percent of the gobbling and hen talk occurs in the hour surrounding sunrise. It's a turkey version of a party in the woods, with pecking order fights and trash talk amid both toms and hens. There's even—gulp—sex acts. However, if you're late to the woods, you'll miss it all, no vigorous gobbles, no fly-down cackles, no sex—if you're inclined to watch stuff like that.

And that's exactly what happened when I was late the other morning. I mean, nothing happened. Oh, I called in a lonely hen who stayed with me for twenty minutes. While we were clucking, the hen and I, a tom turkey gobbled not far away. But just one gobble. While the hen and I continued to chirp, the gobbler wasn't even impressed by the sound of a real hen. He never said another word. That's what happens when you're late.

Yes, I should have known better. Set the alarm, stupid. Be like the bird, dummy. But hey, I thought I'd arise on time. I thought, well . . . I like Dr. Seuss's explanation: "How did it get so late so soon?"

Turkey Moments to Remember

"I don't turkey hunt because I want to . . . I turkey hunt because I have to."

—Tom Kelly

It was close to roosting time when I paused on a Black Hills hilltop, turned around, and looked down on a meadow below. Oh! A flock of turkeys had wandered into the same meadow I had just left. Dang. With daylight about to fade, I decided to simply watch and anticipate in what ridge of ponderosa pines the birds might be intending to roost for the night.

As I peered through binoculars, I was surprised to see yet another flock of birds on the far side of the meadow, walking single file along the edge of the woods. These birds, too, would eventually mosey up a ridge to spend the night. For the heck of it, I sent a few hen yelps toward the flocks but no gobbles; I just saw stretched necks as the birds heard but ignored my pleadings. It was a beautiful evening, warm and windless. As I watched the birds, first one flock and then the other, the birds on the far side of the field slowly faded into the trees.

And that's when I saw it. "What's that?" I said to nobody. A coyote? Must be a coyote. I strained my eyes to get more detail of a rather large animal. Suddenly the "coyote" gracefully leaped into a stunted oak tree and settled on a branch. What's this? I didn't think a coyote could climb a tree like a cat. A cat? Was I watching a mountain lion? A moment later, the big predator slid back down to the ground and continued following the turkey flock. Then I could easily see the tan body, the long tail: indeed, I was watching a mountain lion—a first for me as a turkey hunter. I was both excited and unnerved. Did I want to be there the next morning, in the dark, making seductive turkey sounds—all by myself?

Oh, how silly of me. It was no secret that the Black Hills has a high population of mountain lions, and nobody yet has been attacked. I returned the next day trying to have eyes in the back of my head. No mountain lion. Instead I killed a nice gobbler and trudged back to the truck . . . sometimes stepping in the old tracks of another turkey hunter with a long, slinking tail. Plus, I bagged a special memory, which is the best hunt of them all.

Now fast-forward to Minnesota's turkey season. I was hunting the beautiful wooded bluffs along the St. Croix River. Hearing nothing—not a gobble, not a hen chirp from sunup to about 8 AM—I paused on a wooded hillside and snuggled into a fallen tree blind. I covered my face with a camo mask and began to scratch hen talk on my Cody slate.

Quickly and silently they appeared, two coyotes, one larger than the other. They ran down the wooded hill, obviously looking for me—I mean, the hen. The smaller coyote, the female, I figured, seemed anxious to find the turkey. She stared at me—where the hen was supposed to be—and then she ranged to my extreme left. There, downwind, she got a whiff of something she didn't like and ran like a gray streak back up the hill and out of sight.

The male coyote didn't seem to know what was going on. Instead of following his mate, he sat down for a few minutes, roughly forty yards away. I decided to play with the coyote's mind. I began squeaking softly like a turkey using my mouth call. I didn't move a muscle. Hearing the soft turkey yelp, the coyote got up and slowly walked my way. Again, I called like a hen. He listened and looked. If I could read his mind, he was curious. I moved my foot. He didn't care. By now, the coyote was standing face-to-face with me at about twelve yards. Since I was playing with his mind, I went all out and started talking. "What the hell are you doing here?" I said. "You'd better get out of here before I shoot you."

A gobbler and Ron, half a century of chasing turkeys.

To my surprise, the coyote merely turned its back to me and sat down. And there for a precious moment, the coyote and I were sitting on the same hillside, looking in the same direction, and both hunting wild turkeys. *Pretty cool*, I thought. Finally my hunting partner trotted away. I got up and walked away too.

Both without a turkey.

Of Mice and Men

Following years of seeking elk steaks and antler decorations, it's only natural that I've become quite an elk hunting expert. Many days and seasons I have spent on Black Mountain in Colorado's Elkhead Mountains soaking up more elk savvy, adding my most recent unsuccessful elk hunt to my other unsuccessful forays. By now, I think I could write a book about the many reasons ordinary people, such as yourselves, are such dismal elk hunters. I'm willing to share this highly sought information as a public service.

Many elk hunts ago, I realized that not shooting a bull elk was actually a contribution to the science of elk hunting. For example, my temper tantrums over botching yet another meeting with a bull elk have become less frequent over the decades. Now I've noticed I can straighten the arrows I've bent over my knees.

If you're still an unsuccessful elk hunter, you should know the mountain peaks in Colorado are much higher now compared to your first elk hunt. I don't know how this happened, but I can tell by listening to my lungs beg for air, which they never used to do. It's obvious elk haunts have moved up into thinner air and my lungs have detected this change. Why is it more difficult to breathe on elk hunts? I wouldn't even guess. Climate change? Terrorists? Both, maybe. Scientists will pooh-pooh these theories, I'm sure. But show me a climatologist who knows anything about running up mountainsides after spooked elk.

Mistakes: I have made them all. The biggest mistake an elk hunter can make—besides not knowing a brown elk from a brown horse—is not staying awake while glassing mountainsides or riding said horse. Sleep deprivation is one of the worst ailments to strike an elk hunter. It's even worse than diarrhea, if you can believe that. Most hunters don't know this because they usually don't sleep through diarrhea, while they do try to sleep through deprivation.

How is sleep lost? The main cause of sleep deprivation is the mountain mouse. In extreme cases, loss of sleep is caused by mountain mice, which is two or more. For most of the year, a mountain mouse is content to live amid rocks and stumps and stuff like that. During elk season, however, the same mountain mouse wants to live where you live. Especially inside a rustic hunting cabin. They must be lonely, these mountain mice.

One morning on an elk hunt long ago, I awoke feeling tired, body aching. Then I realized I hadn't slept much because a mouse had been making all kinds of racket running up and down my pillow. I didn't mind the noise so much, but this mouse didn't have the decency to pick up after itself; a bunch of little black spheres were left behind. Some people call them droppings. I never slept much after that and, of course, didn't get an elk.

If it's not one mouse, it's another. One time a family of mountain pack rats wanted my cabin bedroom. They also wanted my dinner fork, my knife, anything shiny because that's what pack rats do: pack stuff away. I won that battle. I gathered my stuff and left.

On my last elk hunt I probably could have shot a trophy bull elk if the mice hadn't interfered. My guide, a fella named Jim, was trying to concentrate on locating elk, but the mice wouldn't let him. He couldn't rest; he couldn't concentrate. He was determined to restore peace to our hunting shack. I was so inspired I wrote about it.

The Legend of Trapper Jim

At Elkhorn Outfitters there's a hunting guide
With a full-face beard and a horse to ride.
He isn't short and he isn't slim.
But today he's known as Trapper Jim.
It happened one night in a hunting shack
High in the mountains, a range known as Black.
We were tired and worn with no elk hunting tale,
So Jim cooked dinner and poured water in a pail.
"What's that," I said to my Elkhorn guide.
"All the horses been watered; we're done with our ride."
"But there's mice in our cabin," he answered with a grin . . .
So began the legend of Trapper Jim.
'Twas an ol' water bucket not filled to the brim,
With a beer can on an axle so the danged thing would spin.
A stick made a trail for the mice to climb.
Jim said they'd follow each other and die every time.
Good food's hard to find for the mountain mouse,

So they smelled the cheese and rushed to our house.
Yet nobody had a clue about what was to begin.
'Twas a mouse-catchin' record by my guide, Trapper Jim.
First one mouse, then two, and soon there were four.
Five, six, and seven, who'd a thunk there'd be more?
But the trap kept on trapping, oh my what a scene.
When we woke the next morning, Trapper Jim had thirteen.
When my elk hunt was over, only Jim had a story.
He'd set a mouse-trapping record and got all the glory.
So that's the end of my tale of huntin' and such,
Of following Jim and not shooting much.
But he's a mighty fine fella, not short and not slim.
If it's trophy mice you're seekin,' your top guide is Trapper Jim.

True Deer Stand Tales

Sitting in a tree . . .

As a place to contemplate and reflect on one's life, the crotch of an oak tree is likely not preferred by the world's great thinkers. Yet I must recommend such a perch, despite the disbelieving stare I received the other evening from a red squirrel. It was a pleasant late afternoon to scrounge a few acorns and otherwise do what squirrels do. All was fine in the squirrel's world until my presence high in the oak was detected. At which time, the red squirrel scampered up to the crotch of the neighboring oak. First came the long stare. Then the squirrel blurted a loud, rapid-tongued *chit*, its incisors clacking like a stick on a picket fence.

If the red squirrel was sounding a warning to the rest of the forest's dwellers, no one seemed to pay much attention. Birds still chirped and other squirrels went about their business. That's understandable. Red squirrels appear to be hot-tempered, mouthy creatures that scream at their own shadows. Hence, their tirades are mostly ignored, much like the chicken who claimed the sky was falling.

A pair of gray squirrels I was watching merely continued their mad hopping through the fallen leaves, making more snaps, crackles, and pops than a kid in a bathtub of Rice Krispies. Nervous critters, squirrels. On the ground, they seldom pause for long. I think this behavior is a learned defense against a hawk or owl trying to take aim. Instead, squirrels often skitter across the forest floor, leap upward to the base of a tree, look and listen, and then bound through the Rice Krispies again.

If you're sitting in the tree to ambush a deer, these noisy outbursts by squirrels are very unnerving. Deer footsteps and squirrel antics often sound the same to the human ear. How can that be? I think it's because when you're waiting in the crotch, you WANT to hear a deer.

Let's face it. Being perched in an oak tree with a bow and arrow across your lap can be a very humiliating experience. After all, you're waiting for an animal with superior everything—hearing, smell, speed, and camouflage—and possibly more sense. Such a thought from my lofty perch is unsettling.

Kids play in trees, but adults? Maybe I should climb down? Well, wait: why should kids have all the fun? Besides, I just heard in the distance the raucous cackle of a cock pheasant. When the day's light fades, it's time to roost. The ringneck is one of the few birds I know that feels compelled to say good night.

Time for some serious tree stand thinking now. The deer ought to be moving. At times like this I easily can imagine a nice buck, rising slowly out of its secretive bed and ambling down the trail in my direction. It's not a sin to imagine. Big buck fantasies are not new. I've been sitting in trees for many autumns and for many hours on many deer trails, each looking ideal. Every time the evening shadows turn to gray and the woodland sounds hush, I'd tell myself that a deer is about to appear on the trail.

It happened once, I think. Most of the time the things that come down the trail are bushes and tree stumps. It's amazing how they move like deer at sundown.

Ahh, the whitetail deer. Now there is a marvelous creation. Graceful. Alert. So in tune with its surroundings. Too bad more people never see the whitetail during its finest moments. Whitetails in zoos or tourist deer attractions are cheap imitations. If I was the king, everybody would be required to get within twenty yards of an unabridged wild whitetail. It's not impossible, of course. I once knew a fella from Iowa who wore moccasins in the woods and successfully stalked enough deer to make himself a local legend. I've tried it a few times, but the soft-soled moccasins hurt my feet.

Most human mortals are no match for a whitetail. I've accepted that every deer season as I fail to outwit the deer where I hunt. Oh, sometimes I get lucky; most of the time unlucky. Every deer season I typically see squirrels, hawks, chickadees—everything but deer. One day I told my deer hunting partner, Bud Burger, that I saw migrating geese and swans but no deer. Bud suggested I'd see more deer if I'd look lower.

Yes, but sometimes deer don't exist in the woods. They vanish. And so you're left with needing an excuse to sit in an oak crotch and contemplate and reflect on your life. And watch the tree stumps prance at dusk.

Strangest Deer Story

There is a good reason why I intend to be sleeping at sunrise to start Minnesota's archery deer season. And I suspect my old college hunting partner, Jim, will be snoring away at the same hour. Don't misunderstand. Bowhunting is a supreme challenge, a sport that attracts hunters seeking quality, not meat. If you doubt that, try to get within twenty paces of a whitetail deer sometime. You'll soon settle for the grocery store meat counter.

There was a time when I wouldn't think of missing an opener, the chance to sneak into the woods in predawn darkness and sit for hours in a chosen tree stand with visions of a super buck walking my way. My plans for opening day started months before: practicing, scouting, plotting. Even the fall schedule of college courses was carefully chosen to avoid a conflict with the bow season. Skipping class was an alternative.

Plainly, it would take a collision with a trophy buck to keep us out of the woods on a Saturday opening.

So: it was on a Friday afternoon when Jim and I skipped classes to finish a minor tree stand–building exercise on a well-used deer trail along the Des Moines River. Iowa's bow season would open the next day. Jim carried a hatchet to cut limbs and brush; I had a hammer to nail a few steps onto a tree. With the jobs completed and the sun perched on the hills to the west, we shuffled back toward the car.

Suddenly, out of nowhere, there it was: a mature whitetail buck. It was standing still and staring down its nose in our direction. We froze. The buck looked away, giving us another view of an impressive set of antlers. At any second, I expected the deer to bounce away. They usually do. This one didn't. Jim didn't know what to think. He was looking at the first whitetail he'd ever seen in the wild up close.

"What's the matter with that deer?" Jim asked.

"Oh, he's just curious," I replied.

Bucks do strange things under the rutting moon of autumn. This one was no different. We waved our arms. The buck stared.

We yelled and stamped our feet. The buck stared. "I'll make him run," I said finally, walking straight toward the animal.

To my surprise, the buck started walking toward me. What? The antlers atop his head appeared like a set of steak knives. Something was hanging from one of them. Was it a piece of shedding velvet? The deer moved closer. No, the something on its antler was a piece of rope. Not tangled up: a tied rope! Was I looking at a pet deer?

"Be careful," Jim warned.

The 150-pound buck ambled closer, leaving five yards and an old slumping barbed wire fence between us. The buck stuck its head through the wires, got hooked, and backed off. Nonchalantly, the buck lowered its head again, this time clearing the fence.

At that moment, I discovered the speed at which a buck deer can carry a full-grown man down a timbered hill. The hammer I was carrying was no defense. I dropped it. Instantly, I was centered between the buck's antlers and on my way to a crash landing with an oak tree. I fell to the ground, holding onto the antlers with a death grip. The buck fell with me.

Jim had never seen a wild deer before; he was too stunned to move. I yelled for help. Jim came running to the pileup with his hatchet and took a swipe at the deer's neck. I sensed the buck wanted to get up. I let go of the antlers. The buck leaped up and bounded away.

Stunned, we hobbled out of the woods and reported the incident to a conservation officer. He confirmed our suspicion that the buck was a pet-turned-mean and had been released by its owner.

My shirt was torn, and I had a cut under my right arm. Jim took me to the student infirmary. A crusty old college nurse looked at my wounds. I told her what happened. She thought I got the worst end of a bar brawl.

In time my body healed, but the mental scars remained. I couldn't lose the crazy idea that every buck in the woods would like to do battle. I missed opening day that year. It's difficult to climb into a tree stand without leaving the car.

Nice Bucks Are Trophies Too

Sitting in a deer stand is good for the soul. Most of us know that. However, if you've never done it, if you've never looked like a blaze orange balloon hanging on a tree limb for six hours or more, well, you have my sympathies. It's a wonderful way to think smart or think stupid. And we deer stand types have done both. But there's more to this deer stand ritual. Nifty stuff. Creatures come passing by, unaware—grouse walking in the leaves, chickadees landing on the next branch, ravens squawking their many melodies, red squirrels barking for all the world to hear—the little bastards.

Minnesota's annual deer season—bow or firearm—is special in many ways, but the most special is the whitetail deer itself. If you've only seen deer along roadsides or in suburban woodlots or on deer farms, you have no idea what a unique creature it is, with so many acute senses, all attuned for nature's most basic law: survival. You see and admire such things as you wile away the hours in a tree stand.

As a deer hunter, you eventually watch the seasons roll into years and then decades. My own fascination with whitetails began in high school when I tried to be a bowhunter. Back then, any deer was fair game. Later, I hunted with both bow and firearms, and my fair game slowly evolved from any deer to bucks only and now I guess you could call me a trophy hunter.

The definition of a trophy hunter varies, of course. One definition is you don't shoot very often. And you throw away more license tags unused than used. The definition of a trophy deer is also all over the map. My first buck with a bow was a four-pointer and a very memorable trophy. These days, as I hunker in a deer stand, my definition of a trophy buck is, well, a nice buck, an eight-pointer perhaps or, golly, a ten-pointer or, wow, one of those weird nontypical types.

Today lots of deer hunters speak a different trophy language. Something about total inches and G2s and spreads and such. Why, I'm not even sure what a G3 is. Or what's a G4 for? It's a language that makes me feel uncomfortable. If the G2s don't measure up or if the spread is not wide, the implication is the buck is less than a trophy. I can't agree with that.

Seems I'm not alone. Another deer hunter I know once wrote this: "What happened to the days when any hunter harvested a beautiful animal and savored the memories of hunting companionship, campfires, the mountains and fresh air, and the physical challenges of an elk hunt? The animal is dead. The hunter killed it, and to dishonor that animal because it is lacking in some human-imposed scoring system is ridiculous."

Another hunter wrote this: "I hunt for me. What I consider a trophy has nothing to do with any other scoring system you can name. I don't need to catch the biggest fish, shoot the biggest deer. It's the memories of the hunt, the tales at the dinner table while enjoying the fruit of the kill, or the conversation at the local archery shop that's important to me."

Yet another hunter chimed in with my favorite opinion: "Trophy hunting is the ability to come home with NOTHING, and when you pull the trigger the animal is a trophy to you."

Fair enough. But I also appreciate knowing the story behind record whitetails, and to have records you need a scoring system. Maybe we deer hunters should leave the scoring system alone until it's needed for a Boone and Crockett record.

In the meantime, don't tell me you shot a 150 class whitetail buck. Tell me you shot a really nice buck. And show me a picture of the buck's rack. I promise I'll smile at your success. In the whitetail wars, we deer hunters ought to be happy for each other.

How to Be a Klutz Deer Hunter

A rumor has been circulating around town about me, implying that as a deer hunter, I'm not the klutz I pretend to be. That actually, I'm an awesome deer slayer in the company of Daniel Boone and Davy Crockett. Aaaah shucks. My immediate impulse is to deny these ridiculous charges. However, following some personal reflection and consulting with the *Boy Scout Handbook*, I've decided to confess and take the consequences.

It's the truth.

While a great weight has been lifted from my shoulders, I realize the news of my deer hunting prowess comes as a great shock to the real deer hunting klutzes who long found strength and comfort in reading about my own deer hunting tomfoolery and stumble-bum-ness. I must apologize for misleading you klutzes. I was being kind. All crafty outdoor writers like ~~myself~~ me know that the klutzes (you know who you are) outnumber the savvy hunters who easily gun down their deer with skill, bravado, and machinelike precision.

Why should I write about my own bagged bucks when the sight is foreign to most klutzes? Better I exaggerate about being outfoxed, outwitted, and outlandish while deer hunting. These attributes are something the klutzes will understand. By dwelling on mistakes and miscues in hunting whitetails (which are just quick-footed sheep, genetically speaking), my own reputation as a deer slayer came into doubt, unfortunately. Not that I minded the smirks or caustic comments from successful deer hunters. In my heart, I knew there was some klutz somewhere who was appreciative. And, too, I've always felt sorry for hunters who couldn't outthink an animal that is only a few chromosomes removed from the sheep barns.

For sure, there is room for humility in the sport of hunting. Even Daniel Boone probably missed a bear or two and, no doubt, chuckled about it. Wouldn't be a sport if a hunter never missed or never erred, right? A hunter who fails occasionally also learns respect for the hunted game and their fine-tuned senses.

Klutzes are humble and respectful; we shouldn't forget that. These qualities are admirable, and I've found them worth writing about. However, the next time I write about deer hunting I won't try to pretend that I have endured such miserable failings. The truth is out.

Yes, I got a nice buck whitetail on my last deer hunt. Goes without saying, of course. Could have had one last year too (with a bow and arrow, no less), but I passed up the shot. The buck was too small. The season before that I shot a fat buck for the freezer. For the record, that's three consecutive years of deer slaying success. No sense boring you with more of my deer hunting history. However, I will explain how my woodsman-ship and deer fooling strategies were the keys to nabbing a crafty whitetail.

Read carefully. In brief, I picked out the third pole on the high line, walked westwardly into the woods, spotted two unoccupied deer stands, checked the wind, and picked one of the stands. The buck walked by seventy-five minutes later. Just like I'd planned.

There's more to it, but the klutzes wouldn't understand, I'm afraid. One klutz I know called to tell me he finally shot a deer, although he later learned the buck had escaped a tame deer farm the day before. It was clearly an accident. He said he didn't know it was a pet deer (Hartford was its name), but the incident has him confused about deer hunting.

"Did you get a deer?" he asked me over the phone.

"Yes," I said, matter-of-factly.

There was a long pause. "You've got to be kidding," he said.

"Nope. Just hauled it home. Nice buck."

"Where'd you buy it?" he asked.

Klutzes also can be smartasses.

Greatest Deer Hunting Tale of All

Jim Jordan stared at the fresh deer tracks in the snow. Three, maybe four deer had recently shuffled by, he figured. But one set of hoof marks caught his eye. The snow-molded hooves were huge: the toes splayed outward like the legs of an overloaded chair.

Jordan cradled a .25-20-caliber Winchester in his arms and took a deep breath of cold morning air. If the tracks were any indication, he had crossed paths with a huge whitetail buck. Jordan peered at the tracks again. He had never seen such massive hooves. He knew he had to follow the inviting track. That decision launched him on a bizarre deer hunt that lasted for more than six decades.

The tracks Jim Jordan followed on a November morning in 1914 were made by a world-record whitetail buck. Except Jordan didn't know that. He also didn't know his deer hunting adventure would take sixty years to complete.

Another part of Jordan's story also begins in the 1970s, with *North American Big Game*, the book of official big game records. One of the most coveted records in the book was, of course, the world-record typical whitetail buck. However, the details were sketchy; the book said the record buck came from Sandstone, Minnesota, but the hunter's name was unknown.

For more than sixty years, about the only thing certain about the number-one set of antlers was that they were found at a rummage sale in Sandstone. When Jordan heard of that discovery, he knew the record possibly belonged in his name. He had written down the story of the hunt the day the record buck was killed, and he remembered vividly. But events made him give up hope of being listed in the records.

Several years ago, I wrote a column for the *Minneapolis Tribune* about the mystery of the world-record antlers, pointing out that the hunter's name was unknown. In the column, I wondered if the person who got that deer would ever know the buck was the best in North America. After the story appeared, I got a call from a reader who said the hunter might be an elderly man who lived near the St. Croix River, which flows between Minnesota and Wisconsin. I looked the man up; his name was Jim Jordan. I interviewed Jim

Jordan in 1977 and wrote his story for readers to decide for themselves. Was he or wasn't he the record holder?

To my surprise, my story about Jordan attracted the attention of officials of the North American Big Game Awards Program, administered jointly by the Boone and Crockett Club and the National Rifle Association. They investigated, and in December 1978 the Boone and Crockett Big Game Committee recognized Jordan as the man who shot the record buck.

Now, the rest of the story . . .

It begins on November 20, 1914, a clear, sunny morning in northwestern Wisconsin, a morning that dawned on six inches of new snow over the vast stretches of the region's woods. Jordan, who lived on a small farm near the little town of Danbury, woke up particularly early. He looked out and liked what he saw: his farmyard freshly covered with snow. It was the opening day of Wisconsin's deer season, an event Jordan never missed. He was twenty-two years old, a woodsman, logger, and trapper, and he loved deer hunting most of all.

Jordan hopped out of bed, dressed quickly, and hustled out to the barn to harness his horse to a buggy. He wanted to be ready when Egus Davis rode up. Davis arrived on schedule, unsaddled his horse, and threw his gear into Jordan's buggy. Together, the two quickly headed into Danbury, bought their fifty-cent deer licenses, and turned the horse and buggy southward toward the Yellow River. When they arrived where they wanted to hunt, Jordan tied his buggy horse, and the two hunters headed into the aspen timber on foot. They had hunted in the familiar woodlands during previous deer seasons. Today they planned to hunt together rather than split up; Davis discovered that in the rush to open the deer season, he'd forgotten his hunting knife.

As Jordan anticipated, the hunting conditions were ideal, thanks to the new snow. Quietly, softly, the two trudged toward the Yellow River. They hadn't walked far when Jordan spotted a doe, raised his rifle, and fired. The big doe fell. Davis was elated by the quick success. He suggested they drag the doe back over the short distance to the horse and buggy. But Jordan was impatient. He handed his hunting knife to his friend and said, "Here's my knife. You can have the doe, but you also can take the deer back by yourself. I want to keep going." Davis nodded his approval, and Jordan, minus his hunting knife, headed off by himself.

He hadn't gone far when, up ahead in the virgin snow, he spied a string of pockmarks meandering through the aspen thicket. From a distance, he knew the tracks had been made by deer, and he knew they were fresh because of the overnight snowfall.

His attention was drawn immediately to the set of supersize hoof prints. He couldn't resist the temptation to follow. He checked his Winchester lever-action rifle one more time; it was loaded, but the magazine wasn't full. The buck that made those imprints in the snow might not be far away. He quickened his pace. The fresh deer tracks wandered southward for a few hundred yards and then turned back north toward Danbury and closer to the Soo Line railroad tracks that roughly paralleled the course of the Yellow River. Jordan continued until the deer trail led toward an opening, the railroad right-of-way. The wandering deer—there were three or four sets of tracks, including the giant buck—had probably crossed the railroad and continued, he thought to himself.

Suddenly, Jordan heard the familiar whistle of an oncoming Soo Line freight train. He paused near the open swath in the aspen. A quick glance at the trail told him the deer had not crossed the tracks. The fresh sign ambled along the grassy strip between the tracks and the timber's edge. He had a good, clear view, north and south, on his side of the railroad bed. Still, he couldn't spot the deer that had made the tracks he had been dogging. The train whistled again, still a long way down the track.

Suddenly, just ahead, Jordan saw movement as heads raised up out of the heavy, tall grass along the railroad tracks. The bedded deer were alerted by the oncoming train. There were three deer or four, Jordan wasn't sure. His eyes were already glued to the one that appeared above the snow-laden clumps of grass less than a hundred yards away. It was a huge buck.

Jordan didn't hesitate. He quickly shouldered his .25-caliber Winchester and steadied the iron sights on the buck's neck. The deer remained motionless, listening for the train and unaware of Jordan's presence. The buck was poised, head high, his enormous antlers shining in the sunlight of the cloud-free morning. Jordan squeezed the trigger.

The rifle bucked, but Jordan's eyes never left the huge deer. The does bounded for the jungle of aspen. The buck went in the opposite direction. Jordan fired again, then again. Once more, and that was the last cartridge in the rifle. The speeding buck disappeared.

Jordan was quite sure he'd hit the buck once if not twice. What's more, tracking conditions were still ideal. He figured he'd catch up with that buck again, sooner or later. Sooner, probably, if the animal was seriously wounded.

He quickly picked up the buck's trail. Anxiously he followed the buck's bounding footprints, looking for blood. Then he remembered his empty rifle. He paused and dug frantically in his coat pockets for more ammunition. He had, he discovered, only one more cartridge. His last shot would have to be fired at close range.

Jordan continued to follow the buck's trail. He found blood—not much, but some. He trudged on. The buck seemed to be heading toward the Yellow River. Jordan didn't mind at all, for the river flowed not far from his farmstead. Suddenly, about 150 yards away, he caught a glimpse of the giant whitetail. He raised his rifle, then lowered it. With only one cartridge left, he decided to wait for a closer shot.

The whitetail headed for the river where it turned west. Jordan was not far behind. He now saw the buck most of the time as it stumbled along. At the river's edge, the buck stopped, his massive head and neck arched low above the ground. Jordan continued to close the distance between them. Suddenly, the buck plunged into the shallow river, struggled against the current, and stepped out on the far bank. By that time, Jordan had also reached the river's edge. Alerted, the mighty whitetail raised his head and looked back.

"He looked right at me," Jordan told me years later. "I aimed at the backbone this time because he was such a big deer; I didn't think my rifle could bring him down if I didn't hit him there." Indeed, Jordan's Model 1892 Winchester, firing the pipsqueak .25-20 cartridge, was really inadequate for deer hunting.

Jordan fired his last shot; the huge whitetail collapsed.

Jordan rushed across the shallow river, oblivious to the icy water that poured into his hunting boots. The buck hadn't moved. For the first time, Jordan could take a close look at the marvelous whitetail. Never had he seen such a set of antlers. Never had he seen such a heavy deer. He reached for his hunting knife; then he remembered: he had loaned it to Egus Davis.

No problem, Jordan thought. If his calculations were correct, he wasn't much more than a quarter mile from his farm. He'd walk back to find Davis and get his knife.

Davis had already returned to the farm with the horse and buggy and the doe. Jordan told of his hunting luck. Then he and Davis hurried back toward the river where the big buck had fallen. But when they arrived, there was no buck in sight.

"The buck must have flopped one more time and slid into the river," Jordan explained. "I went down to the bend of the river, and there he was, hung up on a big rock. I waded out in water waist-deep to get to him. Later, it took a whole bunch of us to pull him home. I can't remember if he weighed just a little over four hundred or just under four hundred pounds."

The news of Jordan's mammoth whitetail spread quickly. Neighbors and townsfolk rode out to take a look. One of them was George Van Castle, who lived in Webster, about ten miles south of Danbury. He worked on the Soo Line Railroad, but he also did taxidermy work in his spare time. He greatly admired Jordan's trophy and offered to mount the head for five dollars. Jordan accepted. He'd seen plenty of big bucks, but none as big as his. Van Castle picked up the unskinned head and caught the Soo Line south to his home in Webster. Jordan didn't know it then, but he would not see his prized whitetail trophy again for more than fifty years.

Shortly after Van Castle agreed to mount the head, his wife became sick and died. Troubled by this loss, Van Castle decided to move to Hinckley, Minnesota. But he never told Jordan, who waited for months but heard no word about his mounted trophy. Finally, Jordan made a trip to Webster, where he learned that Van Castle had gone to Hinckley, and so had his mounted whitetail.

Jordan considered making the trip from Danbury to Hinckley to reclaim his deer, but such a trek was not easy. Although the towns were only twenty-five miles apart, they were separated by a long bridgeless stretch of the St. Croix River. Time passed. Eventually, a new bridge across the St. Croix connected Danbury and Hinckley. But by that time, Van Castle had married again and moved to Florida.

"I never heard from Van Castle again," Jordan recalled. He gave up all hope of seeing his whitetail trophy again. He and his wife, Lena, moved to a small acreage near Hinckley, along the Minnesota side of the St. Croix. He was not a young man anymore, and life had not been easy. Still, he hadn't lost his interest in deer hunting. He shot his share of good bucks. Their many racks hung from the rafters of the Jordans' home, and he could easily tell when, where, and how each had been taken. He started collecting deer antlers as a hobby. That hobby led to still another twist of fate.

One day in 1964, a Minnesotan by the name of Robert Ludwig was strolling down Main Street in Sandstone, a small town about eight miles from Hinckley. Ludwig was a shirttail relative of Jordan's, and he also collected antlers. He came to a rummage sale on a vacant corner lot. The goods—dishes, antiques, furniture—were the usual assortment. One item, however, caught his eye. It was an old, dusty, decrepit, mounted deer head. Ludwig looked it over. The mothy head had been stuffed with yellowed newspapers and homemade plaster, and it had been sewed up with twine. But the antlers were magnificent. Ludwig couldn't believe their size. The rack, massive and perfectly shaped with five equal points on a side, was larger than any he had collected.

Ludwig paid three dollars for the head and took it home. His wife was less than overjoyed at his bargain. The mount was beyond repair, but the antlers were huge. Ludwig, a forester, became curious about his three-dollar antlers. He obtained an official form for measuring typical whitetail racks and measured the rack himself. He wasn't sure what the total point score meant, but he sent his results to a St. Paul naturalist, Bernie Fashingbauer, an official measurer for the Boone and Crockett awards program.

Fashingbauer thought Ludwig's measurements must be wrong. If they were right, the rack qualified as a new world-record typical whitetail buck. He contacted Ludwig and arranged to see the big rack and to take his own set of measurements: an unbelievable score of 206 5/8, a world record. The score was submitted to Boone and Crockett officials, who asked for measuring by a panel of experts. The experts came up with the same score. Ludwig had indeed found the new world-record typical whitetail rack. He couldn't wait to tell his friends and relatives—particularly Jim Jordan, since Jordan was also interested in big antlers.

When Ludwig showed off the record rack, Jordan was stunned. It was the same rack he had lost fifty years ago to Van Castle, the taxidermist. Ecstatic about the discovery, Jordan had a picture taken of himself with the record antlers. He showed it to old friends who had seen the head five decades ago. They agreed it looked like the same buck. Ludwig, however, disagreed. Four years later, in 1968, he sold the record head for $1,500 to Charles T. Arnold, a deer antler collector from Nashua, New Hampshire.

Once again, Jordan was separated from his trophy, although he continued to insist it was the same buck he killed in 1914. He also insisted he wasn't interested in any of the money Ludwig received for selling the world-record head.

"I just want to set the record straight," Jordan told me in the fall of 1977. Of course, the record eventually was set straight when the Boone and Crockett Club credited Jordan with killing the world-record whitetail buck. What convinced record officials to recognize Jordan was one major piece of evidence: that boulder in the river. Jordan had said the boulder stopped the buck from floating away. The boulder was still there.

Ironically, Jordan's hunting tale took one more bizarre twist when, in December 1978, it was announced that Jordan was the record hunter. Sadly, Jordan never heard the news. Less than two months before his record claim was officially accepted, Jordan died at the age of eighty-six.

Postscript: In 1993 a new record buck was taken by Milo Hanson, a Saskatchewan hunter, pushing Jordan's deer to number two.

TALES FROM THE SWAMP

First Meeting at the Swamp

The first annual October meeting of the Swamp Lodge members was called to order for no special reason, except to shoot birds and bull. The duck season was underway and the popple leaves were falling fast enough to see beyond a 20-gauge muzzle if and when a ruffed grouse or timberdoodle happened to be rousted.

I am the appointed Swamp Scribe, a position of great responsibility and no pay. Suck it up, the members said. Therefore, the following represents minutes of the first meeting of the Swamp.

As usual, the gathering included invited guests and hangers-on, who were outnumbered by various bird dogs who, according to the bylaws, have complete access to all festivities and may, after a day of hunting, flop down and sprawl out on any section of the lodge carpet they darn well please.

The foregoing Swamp rule was made by Bill (Piston Legs) Rosso and seconded by Lee (I Missed) Felicetta, two Twin Cities nimrods who are also cofounders of the Swamp Lodge and deserve to be recognized for their weak moment resulting in the questionable purchase of an old resort clearly rundown and already dilapidated. Rosso and Felicetta (and assorted relatives) years ago discovered the quaint hideaway on the edge of an alleged trophy fish lake, which was surrounded by aspen thickets allegedly swarming with gray-phase ruffed grouse that the locals refer to as "partridge" when they're sitting, "SOBs" when they're flying.

But I digress and shall continue with a historical sketch of the lodge as it was told to me by Felicetta and others during the evening's first cocktail hour, which continued until new guests were due to arrive two hours later.

As you might imagine, Felicetta recalled how he was overjoyed and deliriously buoyed by his good fortune of co-ownership of three north woods cabins that were beginning to show wear and tear sometime before World War II. Wanting to share his happiness, Felicetta said, he quickly arranged a romantic weekend with his wife spent in the nicer of the three shacks. She examined the premises hurriedly, Felicetta said, and promptly came up with a name for the place. "It's a swamp," she reportedly exclaimed. I'm told the wife of fellow owner, Rosso, also uttered the same comment when she first laid eyes on the mess . . . er, place. Although the catchy name survives to this day, Felicetta confessed that his wife has refused ever to return, despite the installation of new used carpet, mouse controls, and other lodge improvements of about $1.3 million or thereabouts.

The lodge history completed, the conversation turned to the savvy required of hunters and their dogs who seek the revered ol' ruff amid the popple palaces. Felicetta again dominated the conversation, recalling the first time he went grouse hunting and spent the entire day wandering in the dense woods. Besides having a wonderful time, Felicetta said he also was lost, having forgotten to carry a compass. It really was no big deal, Felicetta said, until he discovered that where he left the woods and where he entered the aforementioned woods that day were roughly seventeen miles apart.

Other Swamp members, guests, and hangers-on offered their own versions of lost-and-found grouse hunting until dinner was served. The chef for the day, Todd Johnson, had prepared a special dish, consisting of the day's bag of grouse breast smothered in a cream sauce. Johnson's meal attracted rave reviews, which he accepted modestly, considering, as he said, "I never measure anything." A separate pan of woodcock parts also was on the menu, although the dish was noticeably avoided by most of the hunting clan. This snub reminded me of Coot, my old Lab, who would fetch anything and everything except woodcock.

Rosso warned the Swamp Lodge members, guests, and hangers-on that next year there would be new rules regarding the shooting of woodcock. "We will either impose a fine or you'll have to eat the bird," he said. Most of us groaned until Felicetta said not to worry because his wife loved the bird's dark meat and he might gain favors by returning from the Swamp with a nice supply of bagged timberdoodles.

To cap the evening's festivities, Gary Amluxen, a noted free spirit, demonstrated his wolf-calling abilities and, much to his surprise, attracted a genuine howl from across the alleged trophy fish lake.

The next day, Jeff Farni, a grouse hunter with philosophical tendencies, stumbled on to an abandoned homestead in the woods. Noting a weathered basketball hoop and backboard standing at the edge of the trees, Farni said with a straight face that he might have discovered a Minnesota Timberwolves training camp.

In conclusion, Rosso announced that the next meeting at the Swamp for lodge members, guests, and hangers-on would take place when the aspen leaves turn to gold under the Hunter's Moon and the tasty smell of Jake Beard's egg-whipped pancakes arises over the Swamp.

Back to the Swamp

During a full moon over golden popple tree and at the end of the road beyond Hayslip's Corner, the annual meeting of Swamp Lodge members was called to order by Bill (Piston Legs) Rosso. The time had come, Rosso shouted above the din, to once again admire and pursue the elusive ruffed grouse, which unlike the "ruffled grouse" is a totally different species. Rosso then called for a review of old business, including his new rules regarding potential woodcock mortalities and the need to consume said bird. After that, he said Swamp members could resume debating the O.J. trial and wondering why nobody in California knew that leather gloves shrink when wet.

First item of old business was the old carpet. In the main cabin, it was noted, the carpet cleaning job had been postponed for approximately the tenth season and maybe the postponement should end. Some members objected to the change in tradition. By not cleaning the carpet, member Gary Amluxen argued, the Swamp was actually gathering character, not to mention several seasons' worth of dog hair. Member Jake Beard said he agreed, pointing to the unusual pattern in the carpet that was unique and one of a kind. He added, "A grouse hunting camp is no place to worry about a few boot tracks from ten years ago."

When Piston Legs Rosso asked for other old business, Lee (I Missed) Felicetta stood to ask for clarification regarding the ancestry of Rosso's hunting dog, Gabby, who at the moment was rooting under the kitchen table. Felicetta said he raised the question only because Gabby appeared to be assembled with different parts in the manner of a junkyard dog. Rosso smiled stiffly and snickered, "It's not how a dog looks; it's how a dog hunts." Felicetta pulled his motion and said not a word in retort.

Thus ended the old business, except for another reminder of the Swamp's woodcock rules. Regarding woodcock, Rosso repeated, there was only one commandment: "What thou shooteth must be cleaneth and eateth by thy self."

There being no further old business, Rosso called for new business items, including the day's grouse hunting results. This request opened the floor to the evening's usual exaggerations and braggadocio. Then, Gary Amluxen, who excels at exaggerating, went for a home run. Amluxen announced for all to hear that he had made a grouse kill on the wing at the record range of forty-eight (or was it eighty-four?) yards. He also insisted that this time he was telling the truth. However, there being no witnesses, the claim was cast off for the rest of the evening, except when Amluxen brought it up again.

As it turned out, the day's top grouse gunner, the scattergunner with the right stuff among lodge members, was the official Lodge Scribe. Out of kindness and modesty, he feigned surprise.

Anniversary at the Swamp

In accordance with the Swamp rules, when aspen turns gold in the ruffed grouse coverts, members of the Swamp, including hangers-on, must gather. These are the minutes of the meeting as duly recorded by the Swamp Scribe.

According to the bylaws, after an evening of imbibing and bragging at the Swamp Lodge, there follows the Swamp's annual business meeting where rules are reviewed, revised, or ignored. In addition, cabin bunking assignments are made at this time. This year, it was announced, a computer was being used to select bunkmates to give all members a fair chance at a quiet night's sleep. Let your scribe be the first to say: a computer never heard a tired grouse hunter snore.

Lee (I Missed) Felicetta, who is the Swamp vice chairman, announced that Swamp chairman Bill (Piston Legs) Rosso would not be attending this, the tenth anniversary of Swamp get-togethers. Immediately following the surprise announcement, Swamp members and hangers-on began a long-standing ovation, the first in Swamp history. In the resulting euphoria, a Swamp coup was suggested, during which Rosso would be dumped and replaced by Vice Chair Felicetta. This idea died, however, lacking a second and upon the realization that Felicetta makes a wonderful vice chairman simply because he has so many of said vices.

In other new business, Vice Chair Felicetta said that the Swamp Lodge nightly closing hours were being cut back to midnight, instead of a half hour before sunrise. The change in closing hours was made, he said, for the good of Swamp members. It was noted that the average age of Swamp members had advanced considerably over the years and was quickly approaching that of a seasoned stand of popple trees ready to fall over. Several Swampers booed the decision, in particular Gary (Suds) Amluxen, the dependable life of the party. He's the same member who—in a moment of "what were you thinking?"—named his three Labrador dogs Light, Lick, and Label.

Felicetta also apologized for the deteriorating character of the Swamp Lodge as a result of the new carpeting, which had covered ten years of dog hair and paw tracks. After a short discussion, members agreed that the lodge policy of unlimited access for all hunting dogs would remain unchanged so as to restore the traditional look and odor of the lodge by the next gathering. The only dissenting voice came from Swamp member Don Kendzior, a rare thinking man's Chicago Bears fan. He said he didn't mind sleeping with a few dogs and admittedly had somewhere in his past. But, he complained, "every time I pet a dog I've got to wash my hands before I eat." This objection was quickly overruled when Swamper Rudy Froiland said the problem could be cured by eating with one hand and petting with the other.

Speaking of dogs, member Jeff Farni said it was time the membership dealt with a festering issue that was threatening to destroy the camaraderie enjoyed by the Swamp fraternity. He said it was almost too embarrassing to talk about. The issue? Questionable dog names. Some Swamp dogs had great but confusing names, such as the aforementioned Light, Lick, and Label. There also were Dover and Raven, which are acceptable handles for canine hunting companions. And Rocky, a golden retriever, certainly had a doggy title with the right stuff, especially if a female dog needed attention.

"So who can explain why Felicetta would name his dog Mi-Mi," shouted an unidentified member. Felicetta was clearly surprised by the members' groveling and disgust over the prissy name of his Vizsla (pronounced *pfish-lot*). Quickly, it was moved and seconded that a name change be ordered under the auspices of Robert's Rules. By a majority vote, Swamp members said that Mi-Mi the Vizsla should be renamed more appropriately. Something more macho. "Brutess" perhaps. Or "Ga-Ga." Felicetta said the problem cannot be solved because his wife chose the name Mi-Mi and he was too helpless or too weak to insist on change. He did promise Swamp members, however, that in the future he would yell "Mi-Mi" in a subdued or muffled voice.

The name issue settled, more new business was discussed. To commemorate the tenth annual foray for grouse, Amluxen, the Swamp historian, said he had reviewed the grouse harvest records and found them to be complete, except for two seasons that appear to be missing. For the record, the best season in the Swamp was in 1991, when the membership gathered forty-four birds. A year later the same Swamp gunners bagged an all-time low of seventeen birds. Amluxen said the Swamp's grouse kill records, allowing for exaggeration, closely reflect the DNR's grouse predictions. According to Swamp statistics, the grouse count has been rising since 1993. And the 1996 Swamp hunt will go down as possibly the third-best of all time, with more than thirty birds.

The history updated, Swamp chef Al (Shorty) Beisner leaped onto a kitchen chair to be seen. The chef's sudden appearance inspired another round of applause, especially after he cleared up some Swamp confusion. Beisner said the night's main course was not rock dove (barn pigeon), as some members charged. It was actually breast of Canada goose, which tasted like rock dove, having flown up and down the Mississippi Flyway a number of times before collapsing forever during a Twin Cities early goose hunt. Beisner said he noticed that all Swamp members ate heartily, despite questions about the menu. "That's how I got started cooking," he offered. "Survival of the fittest."

There being no more business, the Swamp meeting was called to a close, and members retired to prepare for the hunt. One by one, members left the lodge with visions of dog points, grouse flushes, and birds in the bag. With that, Felicetta shut off the lodge lights. "Come, Mi-Mi," he said in a low voice.

New Rules at the Swamp

The annual October gathering of Swamp members recently was held to coincide, as usual, with turning popple leaves, frosty mornings, and anticipated flights of ruffed grouse. The Swamp (for those of you who missed the first meeting) is a backwoods collection of barely standing cabins that were acquired for family vacations by Swamp cofounders Bill (Piston Legs) Rosso and Lee (I Missed) Felicetta. While family vacations at the Swamp were never going to happen, Rosso proudly reported that his wife had agreed to spend two hours at the Swamp, her second visit in a decade.

In the main lodge, Rosso greeted the arriving guests, hangers-on, and hunting dogs and immediately announced a new rule change regarding this year's forays into said popple thickets where said birds lurk. If a woodcock happened to be rousted within 20-gauge range, Rosso cautioned, guests and hangers-on ought to hold fire or be prepared for the worst. After reviewing last year's dinner leftovers, Rosso said the management of the Swamp had no choice but to issue a new policy: if you shoot a woodcock, you must eat it. This requirement did not include the bird's puny thighs. However, Rosso insisted, the woodcock's breast was to be eaten, despite the fact the breast matched the color, texture, and flavor of a night crawler.

Therefore, Rosso blathered, any woodcock dispatcher caught snatching a grouse breast for dinner instead of the required selection would be fined ten dollars. The woodcock change of policy was greeted with cheers by Swamp members Todd Peterson, Duane Boyle, and Al Beisner, who regarded a ten-dollar fine a small price to pay to avoid a forkful of cooked timberdoodle. On the contrary, Don Kendzior, who hails from Chicago (where he said they eat anything), suggested our woodcock taste buds might be improved if each breast was served with a case of wine.

In addition, this year's Swamp gathering was dedicated to the memory of Lucky Louie, a Swamp black Lab who also didn't care for woodcock. Louie's friend Gary Amluxen offered a toast: "To man's best friend, and woman's too; to past hunting dogs, and those that are new."

With new business out of the way, Felicetta said he had some old business to discuss, specifically remarks made last year about his choice of hunting dog names and his ability with a shotgun. First of all, he insisted, Mi-Mi is a perfectly good name for a grouse dog. However, he agreed that shouting, "Here Mi-Mi, here Mi-Mi," while charging armed through the woods doesn't exactly match the image.

As for his shotgunning skills, Felicetta said that missing a grouse certainly wasn't anything to be ashamed of but was, in fact, a normal part of the hunt. Thus, he is very normal, he said. In fact, Felicetta continued, shooting and hitting such a fleeting wisp of feathers in an alder thicket could be viewed as an abnormal event. In fact, he shouted, just to prove he was as abnormal as anybody, Felicetta would issue a little challenge for the title: Top Gun of the Swamp.

There was silence in the Swamp. Finally, Swamp member Al Beisner said he would accept the challenge, provided that grouse waylaid on the ground would be counted as a bird waylaid on the wing. "It appears that we have in our midst a closet ground-swatter," Rosso charged. At once ensued a long, loud, and far-ranging debate, during which moments of brilliance and stupidity were offered alternately by the membership. In a particularly lengthy discourse by Amluxen—about lying compasses and such—only his dog, Label, appeared to be paying attention.

Having failed to solve any major issues of the day, Swamp members retired and prepared to take on the grouse coverts come morn. At lunch, Swamp member Bob Stock reported that his dog, Samantha, pointed forty grouse on a nearby trail before the season opened. Somebody said that was great—if you can believe a hunting dog named Samantha.

Latecomers Jeff Farni and Jake Beard finally reached the Swamp with more good news. Beard said he intended to serve homemade lefse for the breakfast finale. And Farni said he wouldn't be blanked on grouse this year. Having bagged two birds earlier, he brought them along.

On the final evening, Swamp members raved over Todd Peterson's gifted skill in preparing butter-fried grouse breast in cream sauce. Offering advice on preparing wild game, Peterson said it was important to train hunting dogs to be soft-mouthed and not chew the game en route to the hunter. "The most hard-mouthed male dog," Peterson instructed, "will drop the bird when slight pressure is applied to the testicle sack." Members of the Swamp said they had no trouble believing it. The vote was unanimous.

Last Time at the Swamp

As the Hunter's Moon rose over Hayslip's Corner and the aspen tops turned to gold, it was time for the annual meeting at the Swamp. For those not acquainted: the Swamp is a cluster of primitive cabins where the road ends and gives way to spruce, alder, and popple thickets—home to the world's greatest game bird, the ruffed grouse. As usual, Swamp Chairman Bill (Piston Legs) Rosso called the meeting to order as various Swamp members and assorted grouse dogs milled about in the Swamp Lodge.

Upon hearing the melodious, bullhorn voice of Chairman Rosso, the membership gave a rousing ovation. This loud acclaim was not normal and might not have happened if the pre-meeting mixer had not lasted so long. Chairman Rosso promised to lead the nightly debates about woodcock ploys, wolf howling techniques, and other worldly issues.

First, however, it was time to review the Swamp rules regarding personal hygiene (minimum and maximum of one shower per week) and taking responsibility for the doo-doo deposited by one's dog in walking paths or on cabin carpets. Member Gary Amluxen objected, contending his Lab, Label, was not only potty-trained but also constipated and therefore not responsible for last night's odor wafting through Cabin 3.

Vice Chair Lee (I Missed) Felicetta raised his hand and asked for a review of a previous year's vote by the membership that required Felicetta to rename his dog. The dog in question is "Mi-Mi," a wonderful Vizsla. But how can any dog be a hard hunter, be grouse smart, and come to such a froufrou name? Felicetta objected. "Look at me," he said. "Nobody walks harder or faster than me to flush the wily grouse. There's not a member here who's been lost as many times as me; nobody has fired more shots at grouse than me. If I can do it, so can Mi-Mi. Plus, Mi-Mi never gets lost." Chairman Rosso offered a compromise: "Perhaps Felicetta should change his name to something more macho." The motion was carried over.

In the order of new business, the status of ruffed grouse populations was discussed. Vice Chair Felicetta said he was disappointed by this year's flush rate. "I'm not seeing the same number of birds, although I am missing the same number," he said. The general consensus was that the grouse coverts had plenty of birds, but the hot weather, leaf cover, and lousy shooting had reduced the bag rate. Not one member objected.

Nevertheless, the annual grouse breast banquet at the Swamp Lodge would go on. Chef Al Beisner had fifteen grouse breasts ready to sauté in browned butter and strange spices. The chef also said he could not guarantee the origin of each and every bird. "Is this a road kill recipe?" he was asked. Beisner declined comment.

The meat mystery however, did not discourage the stampede for the grouse breasts. Rudy Froiland said he must eat quickly to prevent his dog, Rocky, from sexually harassing each and every dog in the Swamp Lodge. The only Swamp member late to the plate was Don Kendzior, whose tardiness was duly noted because Kendzior has never missed a meal. Don said he started losing his appetite this fall when the Chicago Bears pretended to be an NFL franchise.

Vice Chair Felicetta also announced that Swamp member Bob Stock would be absent this year. Inquiring members wanted to know why. Felicetta said that Stock had recently become engaged to be married and therefore was practicing his skills at skipping entire hunting seasons.

Chairman Rosso said it was time to discuss the Top Gun Award, which annually goes to the Swamp Scribe, a mild-mannered and gracious deadeye who always gives credit to his dog, Raven, a canine television star. The nearest contender for Top Gun was Jeff Farni, Esq., who was celebrating his first grouse kill in approximately two and a half grouse seasons, give or take a few. Vice Chair Felicetta said he also deserved Top Gun this year for having shot the most grouse. Normally, this is how one becomes Top Gun. When questioned, however, Felicetta admitted he had been hunting a week longer than other Swamp members. Swamper Amluxen also objected, contending he had the most BPH (birds per hour), having spent five hours in the Swamp Lodge for every hour in the woods. Chairman Rosso finally announced that there would be no Top Gun Award for lack of qualified candidates. Member Jake Beard said he was a witness to Farni's rare shot, after which Farni shouted a number of expletives for all to hear. Nearby members thought Chairman Rosso was calling his dog, Gabby.

There being no further business, it was announced that this could be the final year of the Swamp gathering because the Swamp Lodge was for sale. "Who would buy a swamp?" somebody asked. There was a moment of silence. The Hunter's Moon stood still in the eastern sky. "See you next year," the Swamp members said.

Postscript: Amazingly, somebody did buy the Swamp. In later grouse seasons, Swamp members continued to gather at nearby resorts. But it was never the same.

FATHERS AND DAUGHTERS, FATHERS AND SONS

About Being a Father

The secret to a good life, it's been said, is enjoying the passage of time. For some of us that passage of time includes becoming a parent. In my case, a father.

Once a year in America, we celebrate fathers for being fathers. The idea of a Father's Day, appropriately enough, was inspired by a good father. His name was William Smart. He raised six children alone. In 1910, Smart's daughter Sonora Smart Dodd organized a Father's Day observance in Spokane, Washington, to honor all fathers who are devoted to family. It took a few decades, but Father's Day became an official national holiday in 1972. Fellow fathers: a day to call our own, a day to be appreciated is pretty nice to have. But sometimes we like to look at Father's Day in a different way. One of our duties as a father is to teach our children all about life. However, fathers soon discover that our children also teach us.

In time, fathers also realize sons and daughters are like gifts for happiness. Oh, perhaps not all the time. Fathers and kids can have rough times. Mark Twain said when he was a boy of fourteen his father sometimes was ignorant and stupid. Twain added that when he turned twenty-one he was astonished at how much his father had learned in seven years.

The same is true of daughters. I should know. I have two, Simone and Laura. Nobody warned me they'd grow up so quickly. Young girls to young ladies, just like that. As a father I suppose I should have known, but then fathers aren't perfect. Before Simone and Laura flew the nest, before it was too late, I made a point of sharing my outdoor passions and experiences with my daughters.

Sometimes Simone was willing to go fishing with me. Sometimes Laura was willing to tag along to hunt wild turkeys. There were times when they couldn't or didn't want to join me. I was disappointed, yes, but I also had to understand that my daughters were expanding their world too. They had friends calling. They had things to see and do. That's what growing up is all about.

So I just waited for the next opportunity to hang with my daughters. *Wanna go fishing, Simone? Hey Laura, let's try to catch a bass on a topwater.* Admittedly, I was slow to learn about the finer details of fatherhood. However, one eventually discovers a father's greatest gift to his children is his time.

Fruitless Deer Hunt Quiets Curiosity

For the occasion she chose to wear her new Jordache jeans, her mother's old hiking boots, and a Jones-style hunting hat of her father's size. She glanced in the mirror. It was a nice funky look, which is important when you're ten going on teenage. Important also when the occasion is to tag along on a bowhunting trip for deer with Dad.

Her name is Simone. She's a typical fifth-grader, increasingly aware of the variety, avenues, and puzzles of life. As such, she has repeatedly asked, begged, and argued her case to go on a real deer hunting trip. And so it happened one day in October.

Her father likes to view himself as a reasonable man. He silently acknowledged that sitting on a tree branch with a chatty daughter was not a ploy the whitetail deer would likely ignore. But so what? Just sharing the experience was what mattered, the reasonable father thought.

He was unprepared, however, for the songs on the car radio. Without complaining, he'd discreetly reach for the volume knob to reduce the roar of rock and roll to, say, a conversational level below hearing loss. Quiet would be good. After all, there were things he should explain about bowhunting. About the wily whitetail. About patience. About the joys of sitting on a tree branch.

"Wouldn't it be something if we got a deer," she said, beaming. Her father smiled back, silently. No need to explain that the last time her bowhunting father took a deer with a bow she wasn't even born. "Deer are pretty smart," her father replied. She turned the radio back to deafening.

Finally, the pair reached the hunting grounds and it was time to head into the woods. A giant cottonwood with a massive horizontal branch seemed an ideal setting for a deer ambush for two. Three heavily used deer trails passed nearby with thick brush to the west and a cornfield to the south. "Listen," her father instructed, "deer have really good ears, so we've got to be quiet. And you've got to be still or the deer will see you."

Her father explained that any deer sleeping in the brush might walk past the tree on the way to the cornfield. "Why are they sleeping now?" she asked, referring to the fact that the sun was shining. Her question answered, she climbed deftly onto the tree limb and chose a perch. Her father followed, wondering if adult monkeys have as much trouble following their offspring through the trees.

"Comfortable?" her father whispered.

"Yes," she replied in a full voice.

"Shhhh."

A chilly, stiff wind gusted out of the west.

"Boy, this is boring," she said after being quiet for about two minutes.

"Shhhh."

Five minutes of quiet.

Simone grew up to be an avid bird hunter and dog trainer.

"I'm getting cold," she whispered.

Ten minutes of quiet.

"My butt hurts," she groaned, making a painful face.

"Shhhh."

Five minutes of quiet.

"I'm shivering."

"Shhhh."

Two minutes of quiet.

"Bet you five dollars there aren't any deer around here," she said expertly.

Does a reasonable father argue with a ten-year-old? "Okay," he replied. "Let's get down and sit on the ground by the tree. Maybe you'll be warmer down there." She snuggled between two protective cottonwood trunks. Her father kneeled alongside, his bow far from being ready to shoot.

Snap. Snap.

Then, there it was, appearing like an instant mirage. A deer. A big doe. Fifteen yards away. And then ten yards. The doe stopped, turned her head, and stared. Her head began bobbing up and down as if confused by what she thought she saw. Her nose was searching for a clue to the strange clumps hunkered at the base of the cotton-wood. Nervously, the deer quickly turned and pranced a short distance away. Maybe twenty to twenty-five yards. She stopped again and looked back. Now was the time. The arrow flew.

"You missed," the daughter said in disbelief.

"How could you miss?" she said, disgusted.

"Why didn't you shoot when the deer was close?" she demanded.

Shut up, kid. You owe me five bucks.

Daughters in the Wilderness

I've been clinging to the belief that it's every father's duty to share a wilderness experience with his kids. In my case, my daughters, Simone and Laura. We're fortunate in Minnesota to have the Boundary Waters Canoe Area Wilderness on our northern border.

Simone, the oldest, was the first to follow her father into the boondocks while paddling from the bow of a canoe. The adventure—how shall I put this—aaah, did not go well.

While a BWCAW guide was a valuable assistant, we—the guide and me—planned a trip too long and with too many portages. When the wilderness trip ended, Simone promptly announced her retirement from paddling in the wilds. I can't say that I blame her. Oh, Simone was a trouper, but she also was a beginner. We paddled too far, too hard, and too much. Wind and rain hassled us. There were sneaky black flies around, and her experienced father neglected to warn her about them until the bugs had made hamburger out of the back of her neck.

Someday, I'm hoping, Simone will be proud of her paddling achievements in the BWCAW. However, I'm not holding my breath.

When it was daughter Laura's turn to experience the joys of the wilderness, I was intent on not making the same mistakes that soured her sister. With Ely guide Roger Skraba, we planned only one portage and one lake. We would not be paddling to exhaustion. We could not control the weather, of course. If it rained, Roger had an effective day brightener. "Rain," he said, "is liquid sunshine." Into the BWCAW we went—daughter Laura, her friend Brooke, Roger, and me. No problem. Pitched tents at a nice campsite. All was well. Roger had the wilderness spirit, and it would, I hoped, rub off on Laura and Brooke.

When the morning broke overcast with raindrops and an unseasonable chill in the air, the longest face in our group might have been mine. Was this going to be another introductory wilderness disaster? *Why can't they at least be treated to sunshine first?* I groaned to myself.

Laura and Brooke, both fifteen, were willing to go on the wilderness adventure. "I went into the BWCA with a blank mind and a lot of warnings on how bad the bugs were," Brooke said. Would they think "yuck" weather and the wilderness were one and the same? I didn't know.

"This is the first lesson a wilderness experience teaches," I announced to my companions. They rolled their eyes, which I ignored, continuing: "Life isn't always the way you'd like it to be. I'd like it to be sunny and warm. But it isn't. So you make do."

"Yeah," said Laura, "then maybe you appreciate it more when the sun does shine."

End of conversation. Weather was now a neutral subject. Little did we know that for the next three days, we'd catch glimpses of sunshine between a steady parade of showers.

The rain did slow down the tent caterpillars that were climbing the tent ropes and walls. And despite the rain, the wilderness was capable of teaching life lessons. "When I first started canoeing, I was in a really big hurry, trying to fight the wind. But after a while, I learned to take my time. And it didn't seem to take so long to get somewhere," Laura observed.

Laura and I were paddle mates. We paddled. Not always straight. Around a few bends and islands in Iron Lake, not far from Rebecca Falls. The remote setting suddenly dawned on Laura. "There really aren't any telephone lines, are there?" she said. "No," I said. She seemed to like the answer. Brooke, too, sensed a wilderness moment. "When I first saw the Indian paintings, I knew I couldn't be let down," she noted.

The gray skies were relentless. It rained, off and on, during the day and sometimes all night. But life went on. We tried fishing and sightseeing via the canoe seat. Brooke and Roger went on a blueberry-picking assignment and returned with a supply for the next morning's menu of blueberry pancakes. Roger cooked them under a tarp to avoid the rain. "I thought I didn't like blueberries," Brooke said, "but I like these."

One evening the wind died and a modest sunset performed its boundary waters magic. Laura and I paddled over the quiet waters. She made mention of her own insignificance, about her newfound patience, how her mood had changed in a day. "I think you learn to appreciate the little things in life, like a hot shower. But I guess you learn more about yourself," she said.

After two nights and three days in the BWCAW, the plan was to return to civilization. The decision wasn't exactly unanimous. Brooke said she really wanted a chance to fish more. Laura was yearning to have a closer look at a bald eagle. They both had seen otters and beavers and mother mergansers with their young. While they worried about the presence of black bears, they didn't mind not seeing a bear. Laura said she'd be willing to go into the wilderness again.

I noted she never said when.

Daughter Laura Lee Schara loves to fish but probably not in the BWCAW.

Thinking of Manhood, Sly Fox, and Big Brown Trout

When my testosterone levels first began to rise, the nearest challenge to my oncoming manhood was my father, Harlan. Although I had hairs on my chest, five or six of 'em, I had to concede that my dad, being a carpenter with huge hands tough enough to drive nails, had superior strength in the arms, chest, back, legs, and, well, all over. Me? I figured I was smarter.

This revelation first appeared at roughly the age of thirteen and continued until I reached age sixteen. It faltered the night I convinced my father to let me borrow the family Ford because I was younger than he was and, hence, a safer driver. Dad handed me the car keys, and I walked out to the garage. Moments later, I returned to the house after making a small dent in the front fender after hitting a center post while backing the car out of the garage. The evidence wasn't helpful. Eating your own words is never good.

However, as for my superior brainpower, the fender bender amounted to a small setback. Spurred on by raging hormones, I was determined in my quest to reach manhood and make a mockery of my father's prediction, which was that I would never grow up. One of the first things I tried to do to show maturity was track down a red fox in a snowstorm, squeak like a mouse, and bring the fox into close range for my single-shot .22 Stevens rifle.

As it turned out, the fox had other ideas. I never did walk down a fox with my .22, and worse, my dad came home from work one day and said he got a fox with nothing but his hammer. True. Well, a barbed-wire fence actually snagged the poor fox; Dad just did the humane thing and put the fox out of its misery. But I couldn't deny that he had a fox to his credit and I had none.

In the race to be macho, my dad was in the lead, although I'm not sure he knew we were competing. Since I was considerably smarter, our next contest would see who could catch the smartest fish of them all, those big brown trout lurking in the Yellow River.

Back in BT (before testosterone), my uncle Bob Dickens recognized that I had a natural ability to be smarter than a trout. All I needed, Uncle Bob said, was a little experience, a fly rod, and hip boots that didn't leak. One day Uncle Bob gave me one of his old bamboo fly rods, a four-piece beauty with just a small crack in the tip. It was made in Japan. Uncle Bob and I shared the same dream about catching big brown trout, the smartest fish of them all. Actually, I was the only one still dreaming. Uncle Bob always caught lots of big browns, most of them just after he said I could have the next cast. Uncle Bob knew I was patient. He said if I kept fly-fishing, sooner or later, some big ol' brown would latch on to my Royal Coachman fly, the one with missing feathers Uncle Bob gave me for a birthday present.

I was still waiting for my big brown trout the day my dad came home with his. Oh, it was a beautiful fish, a twenty-incher or more. Dad was all smiles holding that fish. I remember wishing I could be happy for him. "How'd you catch it?" I sneered, figuring he tossed a gob of worms. Dad went into his story, taking way too long and adding way too many details.

He said he parked his truck along the road and took six steps to reach the big trout hole under the river bridge. First, he weaved a worm on his hook and easily caught a creek chub for bait. Next, he thunked the chub on the head and sliced off a piece of chub meat as if he was fishing for some low thing like bullheads or catfish. Next, he plunked that gob of cut bait into the deep hole under the bridge, and well, the rest is history. Mi'gawd, catching an awesome brown trout on a slab of chub? Rookie luck, no doubt.

Meanwhile, there I am, a picture of piscatorial brains, clad in leaky hip boots and flinging graceful curls on the backcast and watching my tattered Royal Coachman fall on a well-timed mend to drift perfectly toward the big brown hangouts. And I catch nothing.

To this day I'm a little sensitive about the subject of catching big brown trout. If you happen to catch a trout, and if it's a big ol' brown, please, I don't wanna hear.

My Dad's Leaky Boat

The first boat my father ever bought was a sixteen-foot Thompson, an all-wood fishing boat with bench seats and a small varnished deck. That he bought a boat at all was a complete surprise. Although Dad loved to fish, he was self-employed, which meant six-day workweeks and no vacations. Our family fishing outings consisted of a Sunday drive to an Iowa town on the Mississippi River like Marquette or Lansing or sometimes Harpers Ferry. Always, we fished from the river's bank. The Thompson was a used model but not too badly abused. And my father, being a skilled woodworker, patched and painted the old boat back to near-classic condition.

Next, he bought a new five-horse Corsair outboard from my uncle Ray, who was a Skelly fuel dealer. Don't know why Skelly, an oil and gas company, was also selling Corsair outboards, but I don't think the idea lasted very long.

In the summer on various Sunday mornings, we'd launch the Thompson into the Mississippi River at Marquette and chug through the island channels in search of fishy haunts, especially bluegill hideouts. One day we pulled up to shore and my mother reached for a rotting tree stump, intending to tie the boat; suddenly she turned to us and, sporting a wide grin, held up a small Indian arrowhead she had found lodged in the old stump. It was in perfect condition, and we all wondered who made the stone point and how it became stuck in the stump. The story was known only to the river and the tree, and they weren't talking.

While beautifully crafted, the hull design on the old Thompson was narrow and rounded and clearly not made for standing anglers. For my father, this instability made oncoming waves a matter of concern. He was not a good swimmer, and besides, he loved to worry when we were in a boat. Little did my father know there eventually would be something to worry about.

In the backyard one day, I was shooting my bow and arrows at a hay bale and doing quite well, I thought, at hitting a paper plate at regular intervals from twenty yards or so. My archery skill was based on instinctive shooting; that is to say, I was estimating the arrow's trajectory and final landing place and hoping it would be somewhere in the hay bale. If you practiced and practiced at instinctive shooting, you could become amazingly accurate with bow and arrow. However, relentless practice was not my style. I also never should have set the hay bale so close to the sawhorses upon which my father stored his prized fishing boat. Anyway, all was well—arrow after arrow into the hay bale—when suddenly my instincts blurred for an instant.

The arrow flew. I heard a thud. It came from the Thompson.

Slowly, I approached the wounded boat. Wow, arrows are powerful penetrators. A perfect hole. Through the hull. Slightly below the waterline. I didn't panic, but I wanted to. With one bad shot, I had changed my father's unsinkable fishing boat to sinkable.

Quickly, I withdrew the evidence. The hole didn't close. This was not good. *If my dad finds the hole, I'm dead*, I thought. *If he finds the hole after launching the boat, we both might be dead.* This situation called for some innovative, emergency hull repair work, and I happened to be prepared. I feverishly chewed a wad of bubble gum until it reached the sticky phase and attached it to the boat. The gum didn't match the hull color, but it did cover the hole. Besides, I was leaving home for college soon. When the gum started leaking, I'd be long gone, I figured.

I never told my father about the errant arrow. Strangely, he never said a word about his leaky boat. Maybe that explains why fathers and children who go boating together have such wonderful relationships.

My Mother the Angler

My mother never was alone on Mother's Day. It wasn't my idea to have the opening of the Minnesota fishing season and Mother's Day on the same weekend. Fact is, I'm against it. Puts a damper on two special occasions, neither of which should have to share top billing. My mother never worried about Mother's Day conflicts like fishing openers, however. She'd knowingly married a fisherman. And she encouraged her first born son to grow up in the angling tradition. Same with the five children who followed. In fact, Mother rather insisted on raising a family of fishing enthusiasts.

It meant more fishing time for her. Our mother, Evelyn, loved fishing. Mother's Day meant she controlled the day's activities as the honored member of the family. Her choice: we're going fishing. Usually this meant we'd get an earlier-than-normal start to drive to the Mississippi River in northeast Iowa near where she was born. We'd also stay longer on the river. Mom took fishing seriously. She'd pack an extra-heavy picnic basket, including a giant bowl of potato salad, bologna sandwiches (summer sausage for Dad), baked beans, potato chips, Jell-O maybe. And for sure a chocolate cake, carried separately in a huge tin.

The family's picnic supplies had to match mother's riverside patience. And both were phenomenal, as I think about it now. Mother grew up in a quaint old river town, Marquette, Iowa, which is nestled between a couple of bluffs along the Mississippi. Wasn't a whole lot for a kid to do in Marquette, except watch switch trains or go fishing. She went fishing.

Nothing fancy. Mother's self-styled fishing technique consisted of heaving a well-sinkered gob of night crawlers into the river. She'd prop her fishing pole up on a rock or cradle the rod in a Y-branched stick she'd poked into the sand. Then she'd sit down and watch for a nibble. And watch and watch. Like the river itself, Mother seldom was in a rush. She'd guard her fishing pole for hours. Mother never explained, and sadly I never asked, what she got out of life while she sat on the riverbank. Whatever it was, it must have been good.

Oh, she'd catch fish. My, yes. If the family had any fishing luck, Mother usually had most of it. The Mississippi harbors a smorgasbord of fish, from carp to smallmouth bass, sheepshead to walleyes. And a night crawler would attract them all. Didn't bother Mother what she caught. She had an infectious laugh, and any fish—game fish or rough fish—was cause for her to celebrate. A tight line always brightened her day. And ours.

At the time, her love of fishing made her unique. Women weren't encouraged to participate in such so-called masculine pastimes. Fishing was what men and boys did. If Mother was ever told that, she didn't listen. She carried her own night crawlers, baited her own hook, and handled her own fish, dispelling those foolish stereotypes about women anglers who eek and squeal at wiggly things. She'd fit right in today. More and more women have discovered fishing. In Minnesota, an estimated thirty-five percent of the state's 1.2 million licensed anglers are women. For sure, she'd join Women Anglers of Minnesota, which sponsors fishing seminars and trips for members.

On our last fishing trip together, Mother had her usual gob of night crawlers, weighted by a couple of ounces of lead sinkers. "You will not catch walleyes in Mille Lacs with that much junk on the end of your line," I instructed.

"You just watch," she replied. Neither the overload of sinkers on her line nor the cancer in her body prevented her from catching the most fish.

And I can still hear her laughing about it.

Postscript: Evelyn Laura Dickens died of cancer on February 8, 1975, at the age of fifty-five. She was a mother of six: Ron, Mary Jane, Robert, Rick, Roger, and Deann. We all inherited her love of fishing.

Back to Gordon's Woods

Slowly, they shuffled down the forest trail. Father and son. Bits of sunshine sprinkled through the foliage and danced around the first falling leaves of autumn. Up ahead, blue jays were screeching up a fuss over something. Maybe nothing. Of all birdsong, the blue jay's voice may be quite accurately termed obnoxious.

But they—the father and son—ambled on silently. Words weren't necessary. Not when you have common thoughts about returning to a place called Gordon's Woods. As a woodland, Gordon's Woods was nothing special. Just a block of timber along a road of dusty limestone gravel north of Postville, Iowa. Nobody by the name of Gordon has held the deed to Gordon's Woods for a couple of decades or more. But the name lingers on.

I never knew Gordon, but I knew the man who eventually bought the property. He didn't buy the trees to have a place to hunt squirrels or morel mushrooms. One day a commercial logging operation moved into Gordon's Woods with chain saws. When the massacre was over, the loggers piled the heart of Gordon's Woods onto trucks and drove away.

Two more hearts also went with the tree carcasses when the trucks left. Gordon's Woods had been a special place for the father and son. There was no warning before the chain saws arrived. Nobody knew Gordon's Woods was the place where a father and teenage son walked or paused amid giant elms and mighty oaks and an occasional stately American walnut tree. A trail through the woods provided the perfect rustic touch, the right setting for a father to introduce his son to the fine art of squirrel hunting. We sat on stumps and learned other things as well, such as the sounds of the forest. Sometimes, quietly, we'd chat about subjects that fathers and sons find awkward to discuss around the house.

One of our favorite sitting logs was well worn and ideally situated under the far-reaching branches of the grandest walnut tree in the woods. No finer arrangements could be found. The log seat comfortably soothed the father's tired legs and eased the boy's impatient energy. The log also was the perfect ambush site as the forest's squirrels were attracted to the giant walnut tree and its prized fruit. The father and son could hunt and listen and talk.

And they could remember. This was the spot where the son nervously took aim with a single-shot .22 rifle and bagged his first game animal, a gray squirrel. Looking back, it was a miracle of sorts. The son that day also learned about field dressing and caring for the animal that was not to go to waste. Squirrel meat was to be enjoyed.

Aaah, the memories. When the chain saws went silent, memories were all that was left of Gordon's Woods. All the big trees—homes to the squirrels, owls, and birds—were gone. The grand walnut, too, had been leveled. On the day the father and son returned to Gordon's Woods, it was like visiting an old friend no longer recognized. The old trail had vanished, and the new road through the woods was not familiar. But around the bend, a memory was jogged.

A twisted, sad-looking trunk of what had been a giant oak was still standing. Even the loggers had showed mercy for this grotesque, hollow hulk. But father and son remembered it well for it always had been a poor excuse for a tree. What's more, the old oak used to stand near the giant walnut. The father and son looked around. There. Over there. A stump. The father took out his ever-handy jackknife and tenderly sliced a piece of wood from the stump's rotting sides. Then another piece. Under the weathered surface, the wood grain was better preserved.

"That's the walnut tree," said the father. Father and son stood silently next to where the giant walnut had once reached for the sky. Almost two decades had passed since they last visited Gordon's Woods together. No, it wasn't the same now with the trees gone.

Yet the woodland showed signs of recovering. New tree saplings were abundant. Someday, maybe, Gordon's Woods would be a place to go to hunt a squirrel or find a morel mushroom. It was nice to know that. Together. Father and son.

His Last Opening Day

He always had a special fondness for opening day. Opening day was a traditional family get-together and a time to bask in the hopes and anticipation that come with another Minnesota fishing season. He wasn't unusual; thousands of other anglers share the same feelings.

However, this opener was going to be different. Probably it would be his last opening day, the doctors said. His body was infested with cancer, and modern medicine couldn't stop it. Mayo doctors have frank conversations with cancer patients these days. If the medical experts have learned anything about the disease, it's that honesty is usually the best policy. There was a little optimism. Predicting his time of death, the doctors said, was still only a guess. They estimated about six months to live, maybe more, maybe less.

He sometimes was glad that he knew. Other times, he wished he didn't. In a different way, perhaps he really knew his fate all along. He'd been talking about the 1981 opening day for months. He thought about it every day. He'd even dream about it. Since the previous August, when his health troubles started, his greatest worry was that he wouldn't feel better by the time Minnesota's fishing season opened. That was before he was told that his cancerous pancreas couldn't be cured. Not by doctors, anyway.

On the eve of opening day he arrived at the gathering but feeling pain. Not too bad, he insisted. He ignored the obvious differences from past opening days: his inability to help launch the boat, to bait his own hook, to be in every way one of the boys. No matter; he was there for opening day.

Fishing always was a high priority in his life. He found something in the sport that nourished his soul, something that kept him seeking more time in a boat. His patience at holding a fishing rod was extraordinary. Almost to a fault: he often tended to stay in one fishless spot too long. However, his stick-to-itiveness was an asset in another of his favorite pastimes, squirrel hunting. He could occupy a forest stump for hours, scanning the treetops for the flick of a bushy tail. His idea of a "proper" squirrel hunt was to carry a .22 rifle rather than a shotgun. The rifle, he said, required more

Ron's dad, Harlan Schara, with a trophy northern pike.

of the hunter, more marksmanship and stalking skills. It might be easier to hit a running squirrel with a shotgun, he noted, but the art of stalking and the value of patience are often lost.

He established some other hunting rules for his sons. You don't shoot into leafy squirrel nests on the hunch that the nest is occupied. You might unnecessarily wound and lose a squirrel. You shoot only at squirrels you see, and you shoot for the head. The result a good hunter wants is a clean, quick kill with none of the meat ruined. He despised wasting wild game. He insisted that his squirrels be skinned and gutted immediately.

His message was about the ethics of hunting, although he never mentioned ethics. *Ethic* was a word that probably wasn't taught when he finished school in the eighth grade. Right or wrong, he chose to pass on his values, his way of hunting and fishing. His students were his sons. And he spent time sitting on a stump or in a fishing boat with each of them.

Nobody said as much, but now—unless the medical experts were wrong—he would attend his last opening day with his students. He remained the teacher, however. And he could laugh and joke when his sons wanted to cry. Despite everything, his enthusiasm for fishing remained unchanged. He showed patience. He loved waiting for a bite. Even when the walleyes wouldn't comply.

Before it's too late: thanks for the lessons, Dad.

Postscript: Two months later, on July 20, 1981, Harlan Charles Schara, father of Ron, Mary Jane, Robert, Rick, Roger, and Deann, died of cancer at age sixty-seven. The 1981 opener, indeed, turned out to be his last fishing trip.

Don't Let the Old Man In

There's no rehearsal for aging gracefully, although sooner or later we all go onstage. We might become philosophical like Frank Lloyd Wright, who wrote that getting older is "more beautiful." Sophia Loren once observed, "There is a fountain of youth; it's in your mind, your talents, the creativity you bring to life and the lives of people you love." I like that idea. It's also been said there are five stages in a hunter's life: as hunters age their hunting values change. There is proof of that: it's happened to me. It'll happen to you. Maybe it has already.

The first stage of a hunter is simply shooting. Shooting is what we seek. We like to pull the trigger; we pull when we shouldn't. A first-stage hunter is apt to fire off three rounds at a flying ringneck that was already out of range before the first shot. It's okay; don't worry. We learn; we evolve to more advanced stages. Soon we're satisfied with bag limits. Then we seek greater challenges by restricting or limiting ourselves, such as hunting with bow and arrow. When limits aren't as important, we hold out for a trophy. No trophy; no kill.

The fifth stage, they say, is a sportsman or sportswoman. Hunters become conservationists, although I'd argue the conservation ethic begins to appear (sometimes gradually, sometimes suddenly) during the course of a hunter's life. We all eventually reach that stage where our first concern is sustaining game species in a world of declining habitat.

Now I'm wondering if there is a sixth stage in a hunter's life. The thought came to mind while I was sitting in a tree stand on a chilly opening of the Minnesota deer season. Oh, the day began in traditional style: Reached the tree stand before daylight. Loaded the .270. Poured a small cup of hot coffee. Settled in. Thus I began my opening day quest to shoot a deer, something I've tried to do now for more than half a century of Minnesota deer seasons.

What might the sixth state look like? It's more challenging now. You realize you're not the hunter you once were. While I listened for the steps of deer walking, I also wondered if I actually could detect a deer with my fading sense of hearing. My right eye is no longer useful, except for tying fishing knots. I'm a one-eyed deer hunter with a set of binoculars that seem impossible to focus. But I know it's operator error. *Nevertheless, I'll get by,* I said to no one.

I checked the time. Wow, only about twenty-five minutes had passed. A pair of young raccoons sauntered along below my stand. They seemed unaware of my presence. They were fun to watch. I checked the time again. No deer yet. How about another cup of coffee?

Soon I realized something else was different that morning. Lack of deer? Nah. Over the years I've sat for days in tree stands without seeing the flick of a white tail. I get it. That's hunting. No, something was different about *me.* I had the patience of a housefly. Was I bored? Time dragged. Would I shoot a nice buck if he appeared? *For sure,* I said to myself. But it also didn't matter if I shot nothing. Okay, so why such a lack of patience? A decade ago I could sit in a deer stand for five hours and enjoy every minute. Why not now?

I think I found the answer. My old deer stand where I spent so many opening days was full of memories, memories to keep my mind occupied and full of anticipation. My new stand had no memories, no anticipation, no reason to hang in there. I climbed down and headed back to the truck.

If there is a sixth stage of a hunter's life, does it mean the hunter quits? Maybe. I did quit that day—but I didn't really want to. Somehow, someway I needed to rekindle my deer hunting passion, but how? And why did my love of deer hunting fade away so suddenly? The answer might be—oddly enough—in a song that was sent to me by an older friend. I didn't ask to hear it; he sent the song for the hell of it.

Country music star Toby Keith wrote and sang "Don't Let the Old Man In." Look it up. Hear it for yourself. I think you'll be glad you did. To paraphrase the song, the old man was knocking on my door on the deer opener. The old man wanted me to be like him. To think "elderly," "useless." To quit being young.

It doesn't have to happen, the song says. You don't have to think old. A line in the song asks: "How old would you be if you didn't know the day you were born?" Good question. Hell, I don't really feel old. Why was I thinking old? The song pleads, "Don't let the old man in." Dang, I won't; I can't.

Another deer season is coming. I plan to attend.

AND SO THE TRAIL ENDS

My Nightclub Act

"I feel a song coming on." The melody flows as if the Broadway tune had passed my lips only yesterday instead of decades ago. We—about twenty-three of us, all former members of the Edgewater Eight singing group—are rehearsing for a "reunion show." It's an odd feeling to rehearse again. So much time has gone by since the Edgewater was the hottest stage show in Minneapolis.

"Let's sing it again right from the top," says music director Bob Hansen. The voices are older, but the sound that enraptured so many audiences at the old Edgewater Inn in Northeast Minneapolis seems unchanged. Magically, the lyrics come back like memories from another time. And another life.

Surprise: my life was not always fishing openers and deer camps, newspaper deadlines and *Minnesota Bound* television shows. My other life was music: Trumpet lessons and singing solos. Dance bands and rock groups. Like the Fendermen, my money song was "Mule Skinner Blues." Later, music scholarships to MacPhail College of Music. Frankly, I was a Perry Como/Andy Williams wannabe. My greatest fantasy was to be a recording star performing in New York nightclubs. My greatest fear was leaving behind my love of hunting and fishing.

I was in my early twenties when, by chance, a trip to Minneapolis led me to an audition in front of Gary Schulz, the Edgewater's musical director. Schulz was a bewhiskered, high-strung director with a keen musical sense. I sang, and he said I had a job: Two shows nightly; three on Saturdays. Sundays off (or "dark," as they say). Pay: $125 a week.

I was a country boy fresh in the city. "Don't get a haircut again until I tell you," Schulz ordered. "You'll be going to a barber named Tim Hawkins." Rehearsals were held above a run-down drugstore somewhere on Cedar Avenue near Seven Corners. I remember thinking it was such an unglamorous location for eight singers who spent their nights under spotlights. The Edgewater Eight was, by Minneapolis standards, the big time of showbiz. My seven colleagues were young and talent-rich—singers, dancers, and stagewise performers who could sell songs ranging from Broadway to Beatles' medleys.

The group's talents and high energy (and Schulz's musical genius) drew audiences nightly to the Edgewater for two decades, starting in October 1962. On weekends, most tables were sold out. There were early and late dinner shows, plus a third performance on Saturday nights for the drinking crowd. The Edgewater was the place to see and be seen. Eric, the maître d', was superb at remembering faces and names. A discreet tip placed in his hand was always good for a table near the stage.

For sure, the nightly shows revived the Edgewater Inn, one of the first restaurants to perch on the banks of the Mississippi River on the corner of Northeast Marshall Street and Lowry Avenue North. But the Edgewater always kept the dining room curtains closed, especially in daylight. The view across the river was mostly piles of junk or rusted buildings ready to fall.

At night, however, the Edgewater shined. The original cast in 1962 included Jackie Posz, Bob Hansen, Lynn Fitch, Jim Mariner, David Crawford, Kathy Watson, Jan Howe, and Judy Frank. Except for the first year, the Edgewater singers were accompanied by pianist Frank Oliveri, who also wrote many arrangements. Hundreds of young singers came and went as Edgewater members. For some, the experience changed their lives. Three couples even got married: Jackie Posz and Bob Hansen, Kathy Watson and Dominic Castino, and Xenia Mirza and Terry Hemsworth.

In 1982, the Edgewater Eight held its last performance. A few alumni went on to musical careers, including Tom Netherton, who sang with the Lawrence Welk Orchestra. Many remain active in music or theater. Some have disappeared. And Schulz, the mastermind behind the Edgewater's patented stage of ladders and its musical energy, has died.

The famous Edgewater Eight singing group, Ron at center with arms spread, Minneapolis, ca. 1967–68.

When the music faded, the audiences left. Today, there's nothing left of the Edgewater Inn but an empty lot and slabs of broken blacktop, faint evidence of where so many songs and ovations once echoed down the river.

Only memories remain. I remember a younger man who—face still painted in makeup, hair sprayed in place—would between shows occasionally walk behind the Edgewater Inn to reach the river to do a little fishing until it was time to return to the stage. Little did he know his casts into the Mississippi were rehearsals for a larger stage and a greater show.

Writing My Own Writing Obit

If you've ever thought about writing your own obituary, think again. It's not easy. Especially if you're still alive. However, I'm happy to report I did it and lived to tell about it. I wrote outdoor columns for the *Minneapolis Star and Tribune* for more than forty years. Then, the day came. It was time to write the last one, a column writer's obituary, so to speak.

Like I said, it wasn't easy. I wondered if reviewing one's past work, one's contributions to the written word, was a good thing to do. I intended the obituary to be awesome without boring people who are alive. And I wanted to avoid any melancholy or sadness because, frankly, those writing years were the best moments of my life—even if I didn't know it at the time.

I also began to realize a writer's life has its ups and downs. I once wrote a fascinating column about a Minnesota farmer who'd won a very important wildlife conservation award. Writers look forward to seeing nice stories like that hit the Sunday paper. That Sunday was different, however, because throughout the entire diatribe, to my horror, I had misspelled the farmer's last name. Who wants to remember stuff like that?

It's also true that over time, a man's fish tend to grow larger, his bucks grow bigger, and his importance to the world inflates. So you'll have to bear with me.

My first story, written in January 1968 for the Sunday Peach section, was a nifty yarn about man's ingenuity coming to the aid of Minnesota's northern pike. In many Minnesota lakes, pike move into connected marshy waters in springtime to spawn. Sometimes, however, water levels drop quickly, and the adult pike and their young are trapped in the shallows, unable to return to deep water. When winter comes, the pike are destined to die from lack of oxygen.

But wait: help was on the way. The fisheries staff at the Department of Natural Resources had launched a widespread pike rescue program, using water pumps to attract the pike into traps, thereby hauling and restocking the pike that nature was intent on destroying. Saving pike seemed like a good thing to do. Years later, however, the DNR's pike rescue operations were cited as one reason so many lakes became overpopulated with stunted pike. Nature may have had a better plan; some pike hatches should perish, perhaps. Looking back can be a good thing. History usually teaches us something.

Writing columns about emotional topics, such as animal rights or gun control, was always difficult. Going into the deal, I knew I'd make one side spit like a nasty cat. Sometimes both sides of the debate disliked my logic.

I once suggested that hunters don't view firearms like others might. Firearms are just tools for hunting that need to be used safely. After one such column, my managing editor called me into his office. He was curious, he said. Since I owned guns, what did I think about killing people? Well, I answered, when I hold a gun I don't think about murder. I think about watching my muzzle so I don't shoot anybody. He seemed pleased.

When I wrote about disappearing wetlands or polluted rivers or bald eagles making comebacks, I was everybody's friend. My goal was always at the very least to be a warning label.

Today wetlands have more friends in high places, but they continue to disappear or degrade. We mistreat our rivers, but maybe not as awfully as, say, forty years ago. Once down to a precious few, nesting bald eagle pairs in Minnesota number the most in four decades. We win some; we need to win more.

I remember the November the Minnesota deer season died. It was 1971. The state's deer population was so low, a hunting season could not be justified. What happened? A combination of severe winters, liberal hunting of does, and years of declining deer habitat eventually caused the collapse. In hindsight, the deer closure turned out to be a good thing. The DNR was forced to try new deer management ideas, and the legislature was forced to give state deer managers the flexibility, budget, and authority—to protect antlerless deer, for example—to restore the herd. Today, some deer hunters and others complain about the pitfalls of having too many does and small bucks. Compared to 1971, it's a good problem to have.

I also remember when there were few, if any, wild turkeys in Minnesota. The native bird was extirpated in the late 1800s. I met my first wild turkey in the Black Hills as a young editor working for South Dakota's Game, Fish, and Parks Department. It was an addictive experience. Arriving in Minnesota, I began to campaign on behalf of wild turkeys in the state's southeast. Hunter-conservationists such as Les Kouba, John Clark, Ken Burglund, Bob Nybo, Ev and Joanie Nelson, Bill Porter, John Beard, DNR's Gary Nelson, and others joined the turkey effort, and in 1975 the first Minnesota chapter of the National Wild Turkey Federation (NWTF) formed. That one chapter raised thousands of dollars to almost singlehandedly finance the start of DNR's turkey trap and transplant program. Today, the state has dozens of NWTF chapters still raising dollars to support the bird.

Of all the turkeys I've known, only a few have been fishing partners. Celebrities almost always appreciate a time to cast.

One day in the Florida Keys I spent an afternoon fishing with Ted Williams, the late, great Red Sox player. It was an unforgettable experience, recounted earlier in this book. Wally Schirra, the astronaut, was a gentleman fisherman with an inquiring mind. A few minutes in the boat with Wally and you began to understand why he was selected for space travel. He had the right stuff; he also was a lucky angler. Jack Lemmon wasn't funny. He enjoyed fishing, and he laughed at my stories.

Minnesota's most famous anglers, Al and Ron Lindner, were unheard-of fishing guides decades ago. One day they invited me to go walleye fishing with them so they could demonstrate a new gizmo. They called it a Lindy Rig. It consisted of a hook, a thirty-six-inch piece of monofilament, a small swivel, and a lead sinker shaped like a shoe. Al, Ron, and I nabbed a limit, eighteen walleyes, that day on Gull Lake.

Upon seeing their invention, I said I could understand how it would help folks catch walleyes. But, I wondered, "Why would anybody buy the Lindy Rig when it seems so easy to make for oneself?" All an angler needed was a hook, slip sinker, and swivel to duplicate the Lindy Rig. Al and Ron said they didn't see that as a problem. Millions of Lindy Rig sales later, they were right.

Mr. Walleye, Gary Roach, also was a rising star decades ago. The first time we fished together we caught nothing. That was probably the last time Mr. Walleye caught nothing. In the early 1970s Gary also won the first bass tournament ever held in Minnesota.

I also tried my hand at tournament fishing. My peak moment

was winning the Burger Bros. Bass Classic on Lakes Calhoun and Cedar and Lake of the Isles. It was a two-day event and attracted the best of the best: Al and Ron Lindner, Ted Capra, Larry Bollig, Gary Lake, and on and on.

Get this: I, a lowly newspaper scribe, beat 'em all. How? Well, I never told this story, but a few weeks before the tournament, my competitor on the *Minneapolis Star*, Joe Hennessey, wrote a yarn about fishing on Lake of the Isles and catching a nice bass near the island. During the tournament, I checked out the island to discover a unique underwater point, which explained how Joe stumbled into his one fish. I caught a limit on that spot and took all the credit.

My fishing stories for my obituary are probably uncountable. I've caught a lot of fish, small, big, and bigger. But I've only quit smoking once. Yes, the first time I went fishing in Alaska was the time I also decided to give up cigarettes. I flew to Anchorage with my fishing rods and a shirt pocket of nicotine gum. That first day was especially painful and full of agony. Lack of a smoke and nicotine? Not exactly. When my first day of fishing ended in Alaska, I had caught nothing. Zero. Zip. Blanked in Alaska. What angler does that? Fortunately, the second day was better, and the third day without smokes was great; the fishing, too, and I haven't had a cigarette since.

Then, there was the time . . .

Well, I've probably started to bore you. Like I said, a well-written obit shouldn't do that. As others before me, I have come to realize that life is a journey, consisting of various trails to take. Some trails seem endless. Other trails eventually reach an end. This trail of outdoor writing, filled with so many giant fish, huge bucks, and glorious sunrises over the swamp, has finally run out of words. Thanks for the company. I ain't dead yet.

Hunting for the Boy

Years of idleness had left a thin layer of dust on the old .22 repeater. Cheerfully, the man picked up his old metal sidekick and wiped it clean. Lots of memories in his hands.

When the man and his rifle were both young, they were almost inseparable during the fall hunting season. They had but one pursuit—squirrel hunting. Squirrels were made for a boy and his .22. Older folks with money took exotic hunts for ringneck pheasants or deer. But the boy didn't care.

Then time passed and the boy—now a man—had a different view of hunting. While the old .22 gathered dust, his new hunting tools were high-powered deer rifles and fancy semiauto shotguns. And he, too, ventured to more romantic hunting adventures.

Then one autumn day the man felt an urge to go back, to revisit the woodlands of his boyhood days, to once again scan the leafy treetops and watch for the flicker of a bushy tail. Squirrel hunting had taught the man much about a sporting ethic—stalking, marksmanship, and conservation. And the old .22 had been through it all and it was going again.

The man ventured to the timbered hills and bluffs of the Mississippi River Valley, much like the oaky woodlands of yesteryear filled with so many hide-and-seek squirrel adventures. Starting down the timber trail, the man recalled those boyhood lessons that had made him one of the best squirrel hunters in school, even if he had to say so himself. *Walk quietly and painfully slow. Stop often and listen. Your ears will find more squirrels than your eyes. Watch the treetops far ahead where unknowing squirrels may be easily spotted. Listen for the scratch of bark or the crunch of a nut or the rustle of leaves.* The man did all these things, but he saw or heard nothing. It was strange, the man thought. His boyhood technique had never failed. Had he picked a poor timber with no food or large den trees or, worse, no squirrels?

A cornfield was ahead. Another old trick came to mind. Squirrels love that human-provided feast, so the man stalked the timber's edge waiting for hungry squirrels to show themselves. Squirrel sign was there. Partially eaten corncobs lay scattered under the trees. *Be patient*, the man reminded himself.

Soon it was time to move on. Choosing a woody ridge with a wide view, the man sat with his trusty .22, looking and listening between the cornfield and the woods. Old familiar sounds returned: the noisy chipmunks, the screeching flicker, the angry blue jays. His eyes flashed once, catching the twirling last fall of a withered oak leaf. For a second, the man thought it was a foolish squirrel. But there were no foolish squirrels. The man saw nothing.

When the boy had hunted, there were no timetables, no schedules. A Saturday hunt was an all-day affair, just get home in time for dinner. However, passing time had also changed the man's carefree schedule. The wife was waiting to go grocery shopping. The baby daughter needed minding. The lawn needed mowing. The man checked his watch. The boy never carried a watch. The watch said it was time to leave the woods.

Lousy hunting, the man mumbled. The boy never got skunked. If he did, he didn't remember. Something was missing. Glumly, the man shuffled out to the car and drove away. He didn't find the squirrels. And he didn't find the boy. They're still on an oak ridge somewhere.

To My Hunting Daughters

It was their idea. Each in their own time, my daughters, Simone and Laura, decided to attend firearm safety classes although they were the only girl among boys. They passed.

Simone, the oldest, joined the Anoka County 4-H shotgun shooting program. There were tears and disappointment. The gun kicked. And the flying clay targets seemed impossible to follow or hit, despite the coaching. She wanted to quit. But she didn't. Shortly after, she busted five clay birds in a row.

Laura also discovered the addiction of clay bird shooting. She took lessons; she worked at her shotgunning skills. She became a good shot. And she graduated to sporting clays, a new and exciting shotgunning game.

As a father, I was merely a catalyst and willing to support whatever pursuit they chose. Sure, I loved to hunt and fish and shoot and watch wildlife. But would they? When we went fishing, I made sure they knew that girls can do anything boys can do. More importantly, when a fish takes the bait, it has no idea who is holding the fishing rod. In other words, girls can fish as well as boys. They believed me. And, by the way, I never regretted not having a son.

Soon, Simone and Laura graduated to bird hunting: pheasants, doves, ducks, and geese.

Why did they—two beautiful women—enter the fraternity of hunting? It's a question worth pondering. The obvious answer—that a parent was a hunter—is not necessarily correct. Some youngsters discover hunting even though their parents are not involved in the sport. Just as some parents hunt but their offspring do not.

No, you can't force a membership into the hunting clan. You can't teach a youngster to enjoy wading into marsh muck, taking rugged hikes, or arising on miserable mornings. Nor can you teach the spirit of the hunt, those face-to-face moments with nature's cycle of life. No, I believe the urge to become a hunter must stem from something else, something that lies within our ancestral roots.

There was a time when, in most societies, a youngster was expected to be a hunter, to be a provider of wild meat. Or at least the boys were. Hunting wasn't for girls. Those days are long gone. Grocery stores and meat markets are the providers now, and the meat has been tamed. So we all go to the store and hunt—for something to eat.

Fortunately, the rules also have changed. Girls are free to do what boys do. My daughters learned that being a hunter is a slow and sometimes not-easy process. They learned gun safety and the importance of marksmanship. They learned not to be a danger to themselves or others in the field. Most importantly, they learned it was only right to develop skill with their weapon to benefit the wild game hunted. You owe it to the game animal. There's another phrase for it: clean kill.

When the kill happens, my daughters had to handle death as every hunter must. Indeed, they hunt with compassion, the one ingredient that makes us the most interesting of all predators. As somebody once said, "In nature, death is seldom gentle or easy, but it remains essential."

If I could wish anything for my daughters, I'd wish they'll take the time to understand more about the habits of their quarry than the mechanics of their firearms. The benefits are twofold: they'll be better hunters, and they'll be better wildlife habitat conservationists. Why memorize muzzle velocities when the bulldozers are clearing the forests or draining the swamp? They must discover that the single key to wildlife survival is the preservation of wildlife habitat—a place to live, eat, and reproduce.

My daughters also will have to defend their role as a hunter. A growing number of well-intentioned people believe that wildlife would live happily ever after if only hunting seasons were simply closed—forever. My daughters will have to answer those erroneous accusations. They must demonstrate by their actions that hunting itself is no threat to wildlife populations.

As naturalist and conservationist John Madson wrote, "The measure of man's success in saving the best parts of the world will be reflected in hunting and fishing. And just as gamefish and wildlife are the truest indicators of a quality natural environment, so our field sports are the truest indicators of quality freedom."

Oh, I could wish them much more. Hunting friends, for example. Sharing duck blinds and deer camps makes for lasting friendships. And I hope they'll pause to contemplate a sunrise in the turkey woods, the honk of geese in the distance, the finality of a falling leaf. The moods of nature reach deep. Hunting is no spectator sport.

Lastly, I'd insist that they not waste the bounty of wild game. We may live in a throwaway society, but this carelessness should not extend into the hunter's world. That goes for hunting gadgets too. Use them sparingly. Gadgets are an ever-present threat to the ethics of hunting or, to use an old-fashioned word, sportsmanship. Remember, the measure of a hunter is not the size of the buck or the weight of the game bag. What counts is how you hunted as a hunter.

Welcome to the hunting fraternity, Simone and Laura. In my presence, you both have experienced the joy of wild turkey hunting, and you both have walked out of the woods with a gobbler over your back. I can think of no greater joy for a hunting father. I can die in peace now.

Laura and Simone, hunting partners.

ACKNOWLEDGMENTS

Saying "thanks" publicly to colleagues, friends, and others who contributed to these pages is akin to walking on thin ice: one false step and it's trouble. As sure as the hazards of thin ice, I'm going to forget a name. I apologize if it's you. Nevertheless, like a foolish winter angler, I will proceed to acknowledge those who touched my life and my days afield.

In no particular order:

Journalism professor James Schwartz of Iowa State University, who spotted in me a writing skill I didn't see. He turned my life in the right direction. I was honored to speak at his funeral. The only disagreement we ever had was over his habit of eating largemouth bass out of Ten Mile Lake. I contended that bass are great for catching but not for consumption. I suspect my ol' prof is in heaven these days having the occasional fish dinner—bass, no doubt.

Early in my journalism career, I met John Larson, who at the time was active in the Minnesota State Archery Association. We clicked and became hunting and fishing buddies. Better yet, John became an accomplished private pilot who was willing to fly me to adventures from Michigan to Ontario to Iowa to South Dakota. What's more, we survived thunderstorms, dead starter batteries in the Cessna, and flying by the seat of our pants. But always, we landed safely.

Dr. Norb Epping, a veterinarian, entered my world the day he made a courtesy call to tell me that he'd just checked a dog with heartworm disease in my neighborhood. Heartworm is spread by mosquitoes. Although I was not a client, Dr. Epping was aware of my Lab, Coot, who often appeared in my outdoor columns. To repay his kindness, I brought Coot into his Coon Rapids clinic to be checked. And—yikes: Coot had a severe, near-fatal case of heartworm, which Dr. Epping successfully treated. For the next five decades our get-togethers were in fishing boats from Gunisao Lake in Manitoba to Wiley Point Lodge in Ontario to Woman Lake in Minnesota.

Gosh, who's next?

As a newbie magazine editor for South Dakota's Department of Game, Fish, and Parks, I saw my first wild turkey with biologist Art Richardson; my first antelope and mule deer with wildlife chief Fred Priewert. They opened my eyes to a wider world of wildlife.

When the *Minneapolis Tribune* called in November 1967, I was asked to come to town for a job interview with *Tribune* sports editor Larry Batson, a gifted writer but also a man of few words when interviewing job candidates. It was awkward. Larry wasn't much of an outdoorsman, and that's a generous description. As the job interview went into the noon hour, I was asked to join him at the Little Wagon bar for lunch. There I met Tony, the bartender, who served us food and a couple of stiff drinks. Maybe more. After that, the interview went great. Later, I learned that my job offer had actually depended on Tony, who constantly asked me questions about fishing to see if I knew what I was talking about. Tony then gave the thumbs-up to Larry. I wrote my first outdoor story in the Sunday paper in January 1968.

It was the start of the perfect job: fishing with Ron Weber and Ray Ostrom, who introduced the Rapala lure to America; working for Chuck and Loral I Delaney, founders of an August ritual, Game Fair, in Anoka. Day after day, my writing duties led to meeting outdoor folks ranging from muskrat trappers to fly fishers, from sports stars to farmer-conservationists. I thank them all.

In about 1994, John Remes and others at KARE-11 asked me to appear in and produce a short outdoor feature once a week for the six o'clock news. The feature was called "Minnesota Bound." Viewers responded, I guess. In February 1995, a half-hour program, *Minnesota Bound*, hit the air on KARE-11 and has never left as I write these words.

One reason for that success is the man who helped launch *Minnesota Bound*: Joe Harewicz—a talented, hardworking videographer/producer who always carried in his pocket a mouth harmonica in case a situation required music. Another key ingredient was Kelly

First year of filming Minnesota Bound *TV show, 1995.*

McDonnell, a young woman I hired to be my assistant. More accurately, Miss Kelly was highly organized and worked tirelessly to keep me pointed in the right direction. By the way, she is still organizing my life two decades later. We were the first *Minnesota Bound* team. Joe shot the video, Kelly maintained the shooting schedule, and I wrote the scripts.

Meanwhile, Raven, the black Labrador wearing her red bandana, was always the star of the show.

A special big thank-you goes out to Lydia Potthoff from the Anoka County Library in Northtown. Lydia took on the task of converting dozens of my newspaper columns into a digital format to be tweaked and edited. I'm forever grateful for her dedication and encouragement.

Ron Schara's Minnesota has been set in Calluna, a typeface designed by Dutch designer Jos Buivenga and released in 2009 through the exljbris font foundry.

Book design by Wendy Holdman.

CPSIA information can be obtained
at www.ICGtesting.com
Printed in the USA
LVHW030032180821
695508LV00005B/842

9 781681 341927